Stories I've Been Told

The Maritime Storytellers
of CBC's
Weekend Mornings

Collected and Edited by

Brian Sutcliffe

Pottersfield Press
Lawrencetown Beach
Nova Scotia, Canada

Cover photo by Lesley Choyce of Ivan Kent and Brian Sutcliffe at Pleasant Point, Nova Scotia.

Canadian Cataloguing in Publication Data

Main entry under title:

Stories I've been told

ISBN 1-895900-25-5

1. Maritime Provinces — Anecdotes.   2. Tales — Maritime Provinces

I. Sutcliffe, Brian

FC2028.S76 1999   971.5   C99-950019-8
F1035.8.S76 1999

Pottersfield Press gratefully acknowledges the ongoing support of the Nova Scotia Department of Education, Cultural Affairs Division, as well as the Canada Council for the Arts. We acknowledge the financial support of the Government of Canada through the Book Publishing Industry Development Program for our publishing activities.

Printed in Canada

THE CANADA COUNCIL   LE CONSEIL DES ARTS
FOR THE ARTS   DU CANADA
SINCE 1957   DEPUIS 1957

Pottersfield Press
Lawrencetown Beach
83 Leslie Road
East Lawrencetown
Nova Scotia Canada B3Z 1P8
To order: telephone 1-800-NIMBUS9 (1-800-646-2879)

Contents

Introduction

This book is, I believe, a tribute to the people of our Maritime provinces. It came about as a result of CBC Radio's *Weekend Mornings With Brian*, a highlight of my broadcasting career.

Of course another highlight was my seventeen years in Cape Breton, especially the thirteen as a music and variety producer. Boy! We had a hundred or more recording sessions a year in that anything-but-state-of-the-art studio — Rita MacNeil, the Barra MacNeils, Laura Smith, Carl MacKenzie, Doug MacPhee, the Men of the Deeps, the Cape Breton Chorale, Howie MacDonald, and so many others.

These were my CBC Radio years in the Maritimes, Sydney and then Halifax for the final nine. I wouldn't have missed a minute of it.

What an opportunity I had. Getting out around the Maritimes and gathering stories and poetry. It started, pretty much, with *Archie Neil's Cape Breton*. Four years of recording music and stories, mostly at his home in Margaree Forks. The food and the drink and the ghosts!

Weekend Mornings With Brian gradually became Maritimers meeting other Maritimers. I was the lucky one in the middle, introducing one to the other. Mostly there was laughter but sometimes a tear would be shed.

I loved the travelling and meeting so many wonderful people. One of my fond memories is a trip to New Brunswick. I was waiting for the ferry to Grand Manan when suddenly a truck drove up. It went past all the vehicles in the lineup and then turned around and started back.

The driver stopped by the van ahead of me, then pulled up to my car.

He hollered over, "You must be Brian Sutcliffe!"

I rolled my window down and replied, "Yes."

"My God," he said, and he got out of the truck. "My name's Austin Richardson. My wife Mary and I listen to your show all the time. Love it."

That's more or less what he said.

Then he handed me two cans of fillet of herring snacks to enjoy and a little bag of homemade molasses cookies from Mary.

I thoroughly enjoyed both and the chat with Austin.

That's the way I found folks to be all around the Maritimes and I could never get enough of travelling and meeting them.

Now, in this little book, you can get to know a few of those storytellers and poets that I met, mainly between 1983 and 1987. They're just like you and they're just like me. That's what makes all of us and this book so special.

Brian Sutcliffe
February, 1999

Dedication

My daughter, Erin, kept telling me I should dedicate this book to someone and I think she was right.

I dedicate it to her for putting up with me telling a lot of sometimes embarrassing stories about her and about her dog, Coo, on *Weekend Mornings*.

I dedicate the book to my wife, Doreen, the Black Pepper Queen. She hated me talking about her on the show but had to put up with it. I like black pepper now, almost as much as she does.

And I dedicate it to my son, Brendan, for the same reasons really. He gave me lots of material for stories with his many girl-friends and shenanigans. Don't think he minded either.

Love the three of you!

Since my storytelling days began in Cape Breton it seems only right that this journey should begin there. These days, Sydney is home to Effie Ryan but in the late 1920s, well, imagine spending your childhood living in a lighthouse.

Effie Ryan

I don't remember the first trip to St. Paul's Island. My parents took me out when I was five weeks old. They were building up the wireless station. At that point, it was called the life saving station and they abolished it to put in the wireless station. My mother and one other lady, from up in Bay St. Lawrence, Katy MacDougall I think it was, cooked and kept house for sixty-two men for the whole summer, while they were building the station and all the dwellings and everything.

We were into Sugarloaf for a couple of winters and then back to the island again as lightkeepers. That took a good part of, I guess about fifteen, sixteen years anyway. Part time up there.

We lived in a section by ourselves more or less. The wireless station was about a mile from where we lived. We lived at the sou'west side of the light and we could see Cape North and Cape St. Lawrence from where we were. The wireless station was down about, I'd say, a mile. Then, another mile on, was the northeast light and fog alarm. We used to make our visits quite regularly. We'd always go for a week when we went to visit.

There was four families living on that island, most of the time, when we lived there. There was the wireless operators in one big boarding house. The wireless officer in charge, he and his family lived in a classy little bungalow. Those two buildings were quite close together. Side by side almost.

It was a very hard walk. Icy roads. Actually, what we had wasn't a road, truly. It was more like a path cut in the rocks and through the woods. And then you'd be right out on the cliff. We used to have to watch where we were going and sometimes we'd have to snowshoe.

We used to go skating. There was a couple of lovely lakes. By one, my dad and a wireless operator built a log cabin. We used to go out and play hockey with a couple of hockey players from Prince Edward Island. One was Big Jimmy Fraser and he didn't appreciate us very much. We were only little kids. But if we weren't there, there was no hockey. Oh, it aggravated him to no end.

We were never scared. Our parents never allowed us to be scared. Our big storms would be thunder and lightning. Tremendous, tremendous thunder and lightning. Sometimes it would be so bad that it would sound like you hit an oil barrel with a big maul. A big heavy hammer. That's how it would crash down.

The lightning would come in on the telephone and it would ring and ring and ring. And the top of the cupboards on the old kitchen stove would crack. There was three cupboards just pretty well split in half. Old black, cast-iron stove. My job was to polish that old thing every week.

Then, the snow storms and the wind. Of course the snow didn't stay very long. We used to get great big drifts of it but it would blow off in the high wind. The wind was horrendous. Just horrendous. As a matter of fact, my sister met one of the weathermen from Halifax who told her that very often they didn't believe my father's weather reports. Sometimes he told us, "I'm not telling them the truth because they won't believe me anyway."

So he'd say it'd be 160, 170 miles o' gales. But it would be beyond what the glass would register.

That old house, you know, you could feel it. The wind. But you knew you were safe! And our bed would be out, probably, a foot from the wall sometimes because the wind would rattle the house so much. That happened several times.

I remember one time we had a very bad rain storm. We had double porches on the house and that water was so deep out there that my dad couldn't keep it out. So he had to drill holes in the floor for the water to run out.

We had what they called a cistern, for the water to run off the roof. It went down a pipe and underneath the house into the cistern. That was pretty good. In the dead of winter when there wasn't rain, quite often, to save water, we had to boil snow and melt it. Yeah, that was quite a job.

My sister was born there. They tried to weigh her on a spring balance, which would weigh over a pound and a half. It couldn't weigh her. So she was less than that. She was a seven month premee and she looked like a peach. She was the colour of a peach. She was all little white fuzz around the face and great big eyes. She just looked like a peach with eyes in it.

Santa Claus happened to be around that day and he brought her in for us to see. This new baby was put into a little fruit basket, all covered up in absorbant cotton. Soon as we saw her, the basket was put right up in the warming closet of the old kitchen stove and that's where she lived. She lived on warm water, boiled water, and castor oil. That was her diet for, I don't know, probably a week. I can't recall just how long that lasted.

Doctor Munroe, from North Sydney, was alerted and came out but the baby was already born. Mum had a midwife, or a lady, with her but she was scared to death. So Mum said, "You go out and stay in the hall. I'll call you when I'm ready."

Mum had to deliver the baby herself.

The baby had jaundice. That's why she looked like a peach. Anyway, she survived. She has, I guess, nine children of her own now. All grown up. Iris says, "I still am a peach!" That's what she says. She grew up to be a beautiful woman.

We lost two little children out there. My mother's babies. Twice they took her off the island on the stretcher. Both premature. They're buried out there. We feel badly that that's the way it is but there was no other way to do it in those days.

The island roads were bad and the boat, the old *N.B. MacLean*, came in as close as they could get to the island in the drift ice. Then the crew put a lifeboat over the side and, of course, they had a stretcher in it. They expected what was happening and they put Mum on the stretcher up at the house.

I remember my father. Must have been horrible for him. There was five of us then and they didn't think she was gonna live to get to North Sydney. So he told us we had to say goodbye to our mother 'cause she may not be coming back. Poor Dad. I can never forget how he looked. Anyway, she came through that and she got along fine.

Two years later the same thing happened. On April Fool's day. At that time of the year, the drift ice was . . . there was tons and tons of it out there. So, what they did was, they took Mum down the bank someway. It took them about an hour to get her from the house to the boat. It was quite a relief when they steamed away.

She was a great fighter.

We loved it out there! When we left, we were heartbroken. Mary and I, we used to say, if there was just some boat going out that way, we'd hop that boat. Especially if we were mad at our mother for something.

We were brought up with just ourselves, more or less, and the wireless operators. In those days, people were much safer than they are today, for some reason. We never knew bad words. We never heard bad talk. Some of the slang you hear today, that was all foreign to us then. We were like dumb buns when we came to the mainland to go to school. People laughed at us because we didn't understand what they were talking about. However, we learned the hard way and got along through. But it was hard on us. I remember someone saying "Hi" to my mother. I thought, "My gosh, that's rude!" You don't say hi to your elders! You say hello or good afternoon.

Mum was very fussy like that. She trained us well, I think. And we were advanced in our school work because they taught us what they could. When we came ashore, to go to school, we went to summer school and we graded four times in a year. So that was a pretty good record!

I was only about seven years old and I was watching the whales. This big whale came up out of the water and when he blew the water up it was just horrendous. It was away beyond anything the other whales did. When he went back down in the water, well, it was just like a big mountain moving in. And it was quite close to the island. When he went down, there was an echo. There wasn't anyone there with me so I ran home and I told my father, "Oh gosh, Daddy, I think I seen Moby Dick!"

And he said, "What did he look like?"

I told him, "He was a big white whale." And how high the water went and so on. I said, "He looked as if somebody put paint marks all over him."

"What colour paint? Was it red or blue?"

I said, "It looked like it was black. Like black paint streaks on him."

He said, "Effie, no more of your tall tales."

My heart was broken. I was so excited over that piece of news and he didn't believe me!

So, all during the rest of the day, I moped around and felt ashamed and sorry and everything else. And the phone rang. It was one of the wireless operators calling Dad to tell him that a freighter, out off the coast, had come in towards the island and they said they spotted Moby Dick off St. Paul's.

Well, when my father came back off the phone, it was him that had the teary eyes. He says, "I'm sorry I didn't believe you. Yes, he's out there. And you know what that black paint was on him? Those are scars from fighting."

So I'm probably the only one in this end of the world that ever saw Moby Dick.

But it was amazing that someone could confirm it for me, you know.

If you weren't a good manager, you'd have some hungry days, I'm thinking. My mother was an excellent manager. In December, around the eighteenth or twentieth, the supply boat would come with the winter supplies, and I wouldn't want to pay for that grocery order now. It would do until the spring. Until July actually, for heavy things. When there was somebody sick or anything and we had to call for the boat, the crew would bring a few supplies, like butter and eggs. Things like that.

But this order was tremendous and it would either come from Charlottetown, DeBlois Brothers, or from Leonard Brothers in North Sydney. There'd be seven or eight barrels of flour. Everything came in barrels. If you didn't have an animal to butcher, which we always did as a rule, there'd be a big cask of corned beef. Probably salt pork. The likes of that. A big hundred gallon cask of molasses, a barrel of apples. Oh, the smell of the apples was wonderful. And a barrel of rolled oats.

If it was cold weather, you could keep the meats and things frozen. They did have ice but, coming down late in the fall like that, the ice wouldn't be ready. You know, to put fresh ice on. So my mother used to have to cook everything and preserve it in Mason jars. She used to preserve halibut and haddock and all those things anyway, to have for the winter. I remember them doing pork and beef. It was delicious when it was done like that! Roasted and then put in the boiler, you know, and steamed.

We had a garden and we had an old horse. He was a clear old devil and we were terrified of him. He was bad and he didn't like us. I don't know why. I think he used to do it to torment my father, maybe, because he was scared to death of my dad.

He was a great big, old clunk of a thing and he used to get us cornered. One day we got into what we call the forge, where they used to shoe him. We shut the door and he come up to that old door. He backed up to it and he kicked it and kicked it and kicked it until, well, we thought we'd have to get up in the rafters if he kicked the door in because he'd kick us to death.

After he'd kick the door so hard, he'd turn around and he'd go to the window and look in at us. And you know what it'd look like, those big eyes. We were so scared. They were twice as big as they shoulda been. Oh my.

My father happened along and he wondered what Charlie was doing, kicking this door in. So Dad let a roar out at him and the old devil took off down the field somewhere. And we got out. My dear, we were scared to death.

Charlie loved water. This morning they were going out to get more ice and he smelt the water out in the lake. He took off, lickety split, out to the hole. The ice broke and he fell in. Drowned in there. They had to leave him there.

When I was ten or eleven, Dad showed me how to light the lamp in the lighthouse, which I did once but not without him being there. I was scared to death of that because it was a mantle that was lit. Kerosene went up to it and you had to light that thing with a match. I was terrified.

Mary and I and I think John too, a foster brother we had, were taught to put the light out. Quite often we did that. That was scary too because that thing would puff! Then make a bang when the light went off. We never knew whether that was the end of it or not. We had to turn off valves and we knew which way to turn them and how many turns.

Our lighthouse wasn't a very high light because it was away up on a bank but we had to climb this iron ladder to get up. We were supposed to put the hatch down too once we got up. Otherwise, we might have got excited and fell down and killed ourselves on the floor.

You want to hear about the big blast? This when I was four-and-a-half. My sister was three-and-a-half. One of the wireless operators loved Mary because she used to holler and jump and screech. And he'd get her going and have a big row going with the kids. She was his buddy and anything she wanted she got from Sandy MacLean.

The men cleaned the old cannon. I think it was eighteen feet long. It was right beside the big house for the life saving crew and for any visitors that would come to the island off shipwrecks. They filled it with bags and rocks and gunpowder and tin cans. Anything they could get to shove in there. And they stuffed bags in it. Then, of course, the fuse was there.

Mary and I were watching all this procedure. They decided they'd better go in and have dinner before they set it off. They'd be sure there'd be no ships within any distance, you know. Well, there wasn't.

In the meantime, Mary went into Mr. MacLean's bedroom and got the matches. We knew how to light the fuse. Well, my goodness, we were petrified of fire so, when we saw the flame running along the fuse, we took off to the woods and hid.

I think there was thirteen of the men that day at the table and, oh my God, I guess the table didn't upset but everything else in the place did. They realized that we were outdoors and they knew it was the cannon but, how it happened, they couldn't figure that one out.

When they ran outdoors, everybody came looking for us. And Dad said, "I'm afraid they're gone." Because we used to ride horse on this thing. Now can you imagine the thought he had in his mind?

Anyway, when we saw how terrified they were and how concerned, we decided we'd better get out there and tell them we're all right.

We came out of the woods and my mother, I can just see her yet, hands up in the air, hollering. Dad, he sat on the ground and he cried! He was so upset. And we got away with it.

Not so easy with Mum. She warned us to the inch of our lives.

Eighty-two panes of glass was broken. And you know, the last time I was on St. Paul's Island, there was still five or six panes of glass with the cracks in it from that time. You can imagine what they had to do. They couldn't get that much glass. There was all kinds of glass out there for emergencies, on account of the wind, but there wasn't near enough. They had to board up windows until the supply boat could bring out more glass. I don't know how they explained it, I'm sure.

We'd get out there on a nice fine day and all of a sudden the wind would come up. Between Bay St. Lawrence and St. Paul's Island the Atlantic Ocean and the Cabot Strait cross. There's a rough place there, oh, it's about three-quarters of a mile and very choppy. The boats would bounce. It was a strange thing. You'd get in the middle of that area and you wouldn't be able to see St. Paul's Island. Dad used to say, "I'm magic! I'm gonna make it disappear." He knew when this was going to happen.

"Well, where are we gonna go then? We going back to Dingwall?"

"No," he said. "We're going back home! I'll bring it back in a little while. I'll think about it."

So, by and by, he'd say, "I'm telling the island to come back."

Sure enough. We'd see the old island coming up!

But it seemed as if there was a concave in the sea. I can't explain that, I'm sure. We watched for that every time.

One time, one of the government boats arrived. The captain had two cats and they were half-grown. They took us aboard the boat and we always went to visit the captain, Mary and I. That was our treat. We saw the cats and, oh, we wanted a cat so bad. They were so pretty. Little grey cats. Anyway, didn't Sandy MacLean, Mary's buddy, steal one of them. He took it ashore and gave it to us.

The supply boat always spent two days unloading the supplies. The coal, the oil and everything. They discovered the cat missing.

So the captain felt pretty bad and nobody thought a thing about anyone taking it.

In the meantime, Sandy said something at the table to one of the other men about having a bobtail cat when they were kids. This guy said, "What's a bobtail cat mean?"

Sandy said, "Well, it doesn't have any tail. The tail is cut off it."

He said, "That must have been awful!"

"Oh no," Sandy said. "That's nothin'!"

So what did we decide to do but we were going to have a bobtail cat. We took the cat up in this back place, where the lifesavers' place used to be, and got the bench axe. Mary held the cat and I cut the tail off it. But we didn't get it short enough. It was only about half-ways off of it. Well, merciful God, the blood was up on the wall, the stairwall. It was all over us. And the cat took off like a bat. Then we tried to tie the cat's tail up and the cat wouldn't leave the bandage on. Oh my. What a mess it was.

So that night, Mum and Dad entertained the captain and two first officers for dinner. And who arrives but Miss Pussy Cat. Walked right through the dining room and, of course, the captain spotted his kitten. His little cat.

He says, "Where in the world? Whatever happened to it?"

No one could tell him what happened to it. He'd probably have a fit.

Anyway, he said, "Well, it's okay. The girls take care of it, they can have it."

But, oh my God, we never lived that one down for a long time. I don't think she liked us too well.

There used to be a lot of ghost stories. Ghosts were always our friends. We were never scared of them.

One time, one of our neighbours was very sick and they called my mother to come to the house to be with her. She had to walk this dark mile alone on Hallowe'en night. They called her around one o'clock in the morning. Mum wasn't scared of anything. Absolutely nothing. Near to where they lived was this old tree with a rope in it. Somebody replaced the rope every few years but a man hung himself there. They used to say, on Hallowe'en, he would kick. Mum said she thought about that but said, "If he kicks me, I'll

14

kick him back!" So anyway, she took the lantern and she took off. Nobody kicked her.

We were never allowed to waste anything. Of course, you couldn't replace it if you did.

I remember one time we wasted something. Mum used to put seven big sifters of flour, four cups in each sifter, in the big mixing pan. And we did that. Put the yeast in it and made the bread. And it wouldn't rise. All day it didn't rise. So we thought, my God, Daddy'll have a fit! But he never did. He never ever scolded us. Anyway, we took it outdoors and buried it beside the road. So that was fine. Nothing was said.

The next evening, when Daddy came home, he saw this funny looking lump in the ground.

"That wasn't there when I went to work this morning!"

He went over, looked at it, and he saw there was something white. So he took a stick and poked it in. He took it out and said, "I knew right away what it was. Dough!"

The sun made the ground warm, so the dough was away up. Imagine, seven sifters of flour! Enough bread for a week for all of us.

There was a lot of little things like that that went on.

I remember my sister making biscuits. I said to Mary, "It's your turn to bake today."

She said, "Okay, I'll make biscuits." So she did.

Mary didn't like cooking. She'd rather be outdoors messing around than in the house cooking.

She put her mix on the bread board and she couldn't roll it out. It was too dry. She said, "Mum, my dough, it's too dry."

"Well," she said, "put a little milk in it then."

So she puts the milk in it.

Then she had to put more flour. Then more milk. And she did that four or five times, until she had a great pile of dough on the board.

Finally she was able to roll them out and cut them. Put the biscuits in the oven and, oh my God, they were like lead. The cow wouldn't even eat them for her. We had to throw them away. That was a big waste.

So that ended Mary's cooking career. She wasn't gonna cook anymore. The old cow walked away from them.

Sunday we had to get washed and dressed up, just as if we were going to church, to sit down and listen to Rev. Alexander Murray pound the pulpit, from Sydney, here on the radio. That was where we got our first church services.

It was routine. You know, you had to have a routine.

But my mother must have been lonely. Lots of times the other two ladies'd be away and she'd be there by herself. You know, nobody to talk to. They used to phone and call one another when they were home.

But everybody had something to do and there was never a time when you didn't have something to do.

I've had nightmares about being out there on St. Paul's Island in the fog. It used to be very foggy and I couldn't get to see anything but fog.

I would have gladly gone back when I was fifteen and sixteen. We would have gone back. But not anymore. Nope. Not anymore.

In another part of Sydney, a neighbourbood known as Ashby, lives another lady you'll be happy to meet. Agnes Johnstone's recollections take us back as far as her teen years, in the 1930s. When it comes to telling a story, Agnes is quite likely to write a poem.

Agnes Johnstone

We had an assignment at the writers' club to write a document on a journey we had taken. In two hundred words or less. So I thought my journey through life was about the most important journey I had ever taken. I felt it would be different because everyone there, twenty-five members, wrote on a journey of travel.

I was very happy. They gave me a standing ovation that evening. We had a retired teacher who used to comment on our work and he said, "That is an A-plus document, Agnes." I was happy.

As a filament in the wind I began my journey
Accompanied by two irreplacable companions,
Namely, love and self-esteem.
I have always kept them within reach as I journeyed
In the sunshine, in the rain, in the fury of winter storm.
We seemed to make it together.
I never dreamed the journey would be so long.
It's been good though.

During my childhood years, every day was an adventure
And each day was filled with happiness rather than sorrow.
That portion of my journey was a real joy.
Then, as I turned the first bend in the road,

Came the glorious and tempting and unforgettable teens.
There is surely an aura about this delicate transition
When, from the point of being totally dependant,
We suddenly become monarch of all of life's challenges.
We have all of the answers to each of the questions.

And that glorious feeling of our first date.
Our first love.
A little heartache too.
But our main concern was trying to have enough time
        to make our grades, our finals, our graduations.
But we did. Great days.
A few rough patches on the road
But I kept in touch with my two travelling companions.
I was never really alone and we seemed to make it together.
That portion of my journey was an unforgettable joy.

Then the road seemed to stretch out wide
With a hill towering and inviting.
So I braced myself for the journey up.
Each step that I took was a step closer to maturity.
I found my first job. Recieved my first pay cheque.
It gave me a feeling of responsibility, which was good.
I once taught a class of grade two students. I loved it.
I didn't care for them being referred to as kids
So I called my group my Weewees. They loved it.
It was rewarding in more ways than just the pay cheque.
During that time in my journey I met a lot of interesting people.
Some of them men, so handsome,
        one glance made your heart turn over.

A few undesirable tenants on the road made the journey
        a bit difficult at times
But, in such instances, I would recall again the potent words
        of my gracious mother.
When I began my journey, to me she said,
"Keep your self-esteem my dear and never become common.
Choose your companions
        and everything else will fall into place."
What power these words held.

Then I met a very special gentleman. Tall, dark and handsome.
We were attending a New Year's Eve party,
        heralding in the new year.
And that was the the highlight of all my journey.
We had a courtship of two years, then we married.
My two travelling companions were still with me.
They fitted nicely into the scene.
My love had two of the same.
We all fused together so well.
We loved together, we shared together.
Raised a family of four beautiful sons.
Shared their childhood, their teen years.
Educated them for their maturity then watched as each one left
        with choices of their own.
And the home was empty again.
Just the two of us, as we began.

Well, we turned to each other and our plans were many
        and our hopes high.
When, at the end of one year, my beloved was called.
I was alone.
All of our lifetime together, my wish had been
        that I would go first.
I had no choice.
The deep heartache and bleak loneliness left me,
        at times, void of a reason to live.
My boys kept in touch, all four of them, and piece by piece
        I began my life again.
Then, as the weeks grew into years, I made it on my own.
As a few years passed and the path began to smoothen out a bit
My first born son was called. Unbelievable sorrow.
The most difficult part of the journey is when you have to say
        goodbye, forever, to those you love.
You feel like quitting.

But there's a stretch of road out there still waiting.
So I shall put on my shoes now and set out again.
But, before I go,
I have a few small comments I would like to leave
With you wonderful young people
        who are just beginning your journey.

Leave nothing to chance. Keep to the right of the road
And try to improve rather than impoverish.
Communicate one with the other rather than condemn.
Take time enough to stop and say hello to someone lonely
And you will find your own cares will become minimal.
Never compromise your values and, above all,
      keep your good name, your greatest treasure.
Once having lost it, all the gold in the world cannot buy it back.
So I'll say bye for now and I wish you well. It's getting late.
I have to set out again and see what's around the bend
      of the road.

I was the youngest of a family of eight and my brother, Paul, he adored poetry. He had all the masters and he used to read to me when I was just school age. I remember a few lines. It took me half a lifetime to finally get the book but he used to read to me.

And then, while round them shadows gathered faster
And as the firelight fell, he read aloud the book
Wherein the master had writ of Little Nell.

And finally I did get a copy of *Little Nell*. So that was the beginning. It was part of our lives. Beautiful music also.

I grew up in Sydney. After my husband died, I travelled just about all over Canada. I spent time with one son in Alberta. I had a friend in Toronto and visited with her and her husband. I went to Vancouver with another lady for a brief period. Then I went to Prince Edward Island with another son and I visited my youngest son who was in Canso at that time.

You can't help but write about nature. Nature is my preference and also events that take place in my life. You know what I mean. Sometimes you're all filled up with sorrow and if you write, sit down and put it into words, it's a great release. That's what I find. And nature, it's so compelling. Especially in Cape Breton.

I was visiting with my son. He had a very beautiful home at Athabaska, Alberta, with two or three acres of land, above the Athabaska River. It was three levels and I had the one near the ground. This tiny little rabbit used to come up to the window. He'd peek right in at me. They're much larger than the rabbits here with big hind legs. He was brown and he was beautiful. I stayed a couple of months. One day it was hopping away and I said to Barry, "In the name of time, that wasn't the same rabbit. All the backs of his legs are white."

My son said, "Yes, he's getting ready for his winter wear. They change to white."

And then it came back to me that they do.

So I sat down and wrote it. I just couldn't help it.

The Little Brown Rabbit In Winter White Wear

Along the road by a quiet wood
I stopped for a moment to take my ease.
The autumn had gone and the brush had turned brown
And I noticed a stirring among the trees.
A little brown rabbit was munching there.
Two shining eyes, all alert and aware
Of every sound in the morning air.

On his hind legs he stood as he ate his fare
And he looked all about in the fallen leaves
For little wild nuts that had fallen there.
And he gathered them up for his harvest sheaves.
Under the gray of the morning skies
His brown summer coat was a wonderful guise.
The very same shade as the rushes tall.
You scarcely could see him there at all.

Along the road, by a quiet wood,
I stopped for a moment to take my ease.
The winter had come and the white snow lay
On every bough of the woodland trees.
The road was white with a bluish shade
All the way down to the everglade
As I looked back at the tracks I had made.

And as I looked back, to my own surprise
Another set of tracks appeared.
And I crossed the road to the other side
To the undergrowth where the branches sheared.
And then I saw him standing there
All newly dressed in his white winter wear.
In a coat of white he looked oh, so fair.
The little brown rabbit I'd written about

21

Only two months before in the everglade fair.
And now, with the coming of winter's white,
A little white rabbit stood munching there.

Under the blue of the winter skies
His winter white coat was a wonderful guise.
The very same shade as the rushes tall
You scarcely could see him there at all.
The wonders of nature triumphant to see.
You ask me a question of how this could be?
I have not the answers to give you. You see,
They come from a much greater Being than me.
The little white rabbit in winter white wear
Will change back to brown when the blossoms appear.

A dear old gentleman used to walk around the neighbourhood every day. He wouldn't say a word. Just smile, bow his head and put his two fingers up. The old sage, I called him. He lived all alone, just up at the end of our street, and everybody thought the world of him. So I called it, "The Old Sage."

While walking down the street one day
I met an old man on the way.
His shoes were worn, his coat was black,
His hands were clasped behind his back.

He nodded as he passed my way
And smiled and bade me time of day.
He did not speak a word and yet
His saga I will not forget.

For in his eyes and wrinkled face,
As varied as the sands we trace,
A history in those eyes I gleaned
Of joys long spent and fortune meaned.
And many sorrows too I'd say
And yet, he smiled and went his way.

While walking down the street today
I met the old man on the way.
His hands still clasped behind his back
A scarf tied round his coat of black.

The wind was stiff, his head was low
And yet he smiled and said hello.
He lives alone I've heard it said.
A stove, a chair, a trundle bed.

Down the long road I watched him go
And felt I'd known him long ago.
As though some other life I'd known.
I claimed the old man for my own.
He does not live alone, my kin
God's angels live next door to him.

Stories that I used to hear, when I was very young, that this old gentleman had lived way out in the Cow Bay Road area. He lived there with his wife and her name was Sarah or something. I don't really know but they called her Sally.

My Cottage In the Valley

When the winter wind is blowing
And it's past the time for hoeing
Then I settle in to take a little rest.
And beside an open fire
Find the peace that I desire
As I watch the crimson sun sink in the west.

In my cottage in the valley,
That once I shared with Sally,
Alone I live with just my memories.
For no one comes to see me
Since my Sally had to leave me.
God took her and she meant the world to me.

She was kind and understanding
And she seemed to take a hand in
Every trial and every task that came my way.
In the night she'd reassure me,
With her smiling face before me,
That the morning sun would bring a brighter day.

Now she's sleeping in the shadow
Of the pine grove in the meadow.
Every day I go to see her when I can.
And I tell her how I love her
And I kiss the earth above her
And it seems I feel her presence once again.

In the morning very early
When the frosted snow is pearly
With my hatchet and my sleigh I set to go
To my woodland grove and stake
Out beyond the frozen lake
Where I split the logs for burning, cord in tow.

I have fuel for my fire,
All the needs that I require,
Books to read and food aplenty in the bin,
In my cottage in the valley
That once I shared with Sally.
I won't rest until I see her once again.

I went out to the lake after years and years. My son took me for a canoe ride, all around the lake. The old apple orchard was still there where this old gentleman was supposed to have lived. Just stories I had heard when I was young and it left an impression on me. I went back in time and I thought about him living there.

I loved the outdoors. Lakes, rivers and walking through the woods. I think that was my favourite. I wrote "The Hermit Thrush." I was up by a little brook that runs down through the old Cossitt property and the thrush began to sing. As you walk along, he goes ahead of you, to distant trees, and he keeps that beautiful song going. It's hauntingly beautiful. I was all alone at the time and it brought back memories of my childhood.

The Hermit Thrush

From a branch by the river I heard a song
Above the soft stir of the underbrush.
The notes echo out clearly as I walk along.
The beautiful song of the hermit thrush.

So sweet yet a small touch of loneliness too.
It filled the deep forest that soft summer morn.
And it seemed to awaken a feeling in me
That too long had been sleeping and memories took form.

I remembered my childhood when I wandered there
With my sisters and brothers and friends that I knew.
And we'd sit by the river and mimic the air
Of the song of the thrush in the soft summer dew.

It still touched my heart, though a child I was then,
How such beautiful notes from his little throat came.
And I clearly remember the echoing sound
That trilled through the forest again and again.

A plain little creature in simple array.
No plumes on his tail and no trim on his wings.
You scarcely would notice him sitting up there
'Til he lifts his sweet voice to God's heaven and sings.

It still touches my heart, though I'm older grown now
And tired of the pace of life's turmoil and rush.
Let me walk at my ease through the woodland and hear
From a branch by the river, the song of the thrush.

My first poem ever written won a competition in grade eleven, at Holy Angels, in 1937. That's a long, long time ago. It was published in several papers. *The Montreal Standard* and all of those. We had to write on our favourite month so I thought spring was the beginning of everything.

Beauties of Spring

Far through the valley the robin is singing
Swelling his note to the fullness of May.
While, from the hilltops, the echoes come ringing
Louder and louder then dying away.

Rivers are gushing and surging and swelling
Glad to be free from their prisons of snow.
Up from the southward the soft winds are telling
Tales of the joys that the world soon shall know.

Green fields and valleys and mists in the morning.
Sweet-scented cherry blooms filling the air.
White clouds of cotton the blue skies adorning.
Where are the beauties with these to compare?

I have one here that I favour. I don't know if it's my special favourite but I certainly favour it. It's about my husband and my son
who died. It was just depicting my feelings. All the things we used to
like. The woods, the lake and the long, winding road.

Separation

I did, with faith, hold tight the strings
With hunger in my heart that day.
For all the love that once had been
I watched, by pieces, slip away.

The man I loved had given to me
Four sons of love beside his own.
And by his side we viewed with pride
Each little face 'til they were grown.

Perplexed the world and sad the beat
Of every lonely, loving heart
When death will separate the two
And tear the loving ties apart.

And separate a mother's love from her first born.
The agony of loss of a beloved son.
Death too has taken part of me.

True love will never pass away
But deeper grows with passing time.
And through the files of memory
Recounts each moment line by line.

I have sixteen poems down for my next book. Hopefully, I'll
live long enough to complete it. You have to have at least twenty-
one. With twenty-one pictures. Around forty-two pages for a pocket
book of verse. That's what they require.

These were the dreams I had when I started out first with my marriage. Of course, we have no choice. When death comes, it comes. But this was our dream at the beginning. I call it

We'll Set Out Together

We'll set out together on life's crowded highway.
I'll be beside you wherever you go.
On through the level, the hills and the bi-way,
We'll walk through the flowers and on through the snow.

Some days the road will rise brilliant before us.
Some days the hills will be rugged to climb.
Some days the load will lie heavy upon us.
Some days we'll drench in the sun's golden shine.

As long as we see in each other the riches
Of love's warm glow, as the years trickle by,
Two hearts, as one, will surmount all the glitches
That clutter the grasses and shadow the sky.

We'll walk on together with a love that will bind us
As each year bids goodbye to an old year again.
When the dreams that we planned and the hills that we climbed
Are just shadows behind us and serenity waits like a soft,
        summer refrain.

We set out together, we'll turn home together.
You'll be beside me at day's gentle close.
God's guiding hand will direct us as whether
We'll walk through the flowers or wait for the snows.

27

From Sydney, let's head for Nova Scotia's Eastern Shore. I always take the old road, Route 4, to the Strait of Canso. There's something about it. You never quite know what beauty lies around the next curve or over the next hill. At Antigonish we turn off and head towards Sherbrooke. We're on Route 7 and just past Salmon River Bridge, we turn left. At the end of the road we've arrived at Pleasant Point. That's where Ivan Kent and his wife Mildred live and run their friendly bed and breakfast.

Ivan Kent

Well, the first one of my family to come here was my great-grandfather, William Thomas Kent. He joined the navy, the British navy, about 1786. He was a midshipman at ten years old, which was common in the British navy then, and became a commissioned officer. He sailed with Admiral Nelson for some years. Admiral Nelson, of course, was in the navy considerable years before that. Brought in nine years old as a midshipman.

He was with Nelson at the Battle of the Nile in 1798. He was also with Nelson when Nelson was killed at Trafalgar in 1805. In 1808, he was transferred here to Halifax which was a British naval base then. I have some records that show he was back in England in April of 1811, then returned to Halifax and married a school teacher. Her name was Elizabeth May. That was an English family. She was born just up the road here about a mile or so but she was teaching in Halifax at the time.

He was involved in the British-American War of 1812. After a skirmish down off of Boston, where they captured an American ship, he was wounded. He had a sword run through his hip. So they brought the ship back to Halifax as a war prize and the American prisoners were put on Melville Island, a prison island at that time. In fact, was so until after the Second World War. And he served as governor of the prison for four or five years. His first two children, Margaret and Robert, were born there.

Then he retired and took his pension. I suppose because his wife's people were living here in the area, he requested a grant of land, which he was entitled to, through this string of islands here. But he couldn't get it. It had already been granted to somebody. So he took a grant east of here about three miles back of the backwater, on a brook. He built a log cabin there for a couple of years. At that time, if you didn't settle it in five years, the grant was lost. The other chap never showed up so Great-grandfather then took over this grant of land that he wanted originally.

He built his first frame house right over there where the lighthouse stands now. About ten feet from there. That's where he brought up his family. My grandfather was his youngest son and he built this house in 1861. My grandfather was the youngest of twelve, my father was the youngest of twelve and I was the youngest of eleven. So they were big families.

My grandfather died in 1908. He was a lightkeeper. That lighthouse was built just at the turn of the century and he was lightkeeper for that short time. Then my father was appointed as lightkeeper. He passed away and my mother was lightkeeper. Of course, we were looking after it.

I remember, when I was pretty young, we'd go over there in the night. Sundown, you had to go over and light the lamp. It was a big, brass, double wick lamp. You trimmed the wicks and got the light burning good. And there was a lotta brass up there at the lantern o' the lighthouse then. That all had to be polished. Then, the glasses all cleaned. The windows. There was two rings on the sides of the lamp and you picked it up with two big hooks. There was a sixteen-candlelight prism there that you set the light down inside of. I always kept a big wooden box there, so I could get up on it to reach the light and get it high enough to lower it down into the lantern. Then in the morning, of course, you had to go over and blow it out at sunrise.

I don't know why we had to keep weather records every day. All the reports were sent in quarterly. And everything had to be accounted for even down to the cleaning rags you used, the gallons of oil and so on. Of course, the light was run by kerosene.

I was the youngest of eleven and all my brothers and sisters were born here in the house. By midwifery mostly, because the doctor was twenty or thirty miles away and had to come by horse team. So he didn't get here 'til, usually, a week after the fact. So there were many women around that were midwives and they looked after things.

But when I was expected, around New Year's, the doctor had told my mother that I was gonna be a bad feller, right from the start, and she'd have to go to a hospital in Halifax.

She stayed here for Christmas day to celebrate as usual and the day after Father arranged for Mother to go to Halifax. Now travel down here in the summertime was mostly by boat, if you went up to the city. We went up on the freighters. You could, in the winter, go up here by horse team and then go in on the train from Musquodoboit Harbour to Dartmouth. But one of the few cars around here at the time was over in the next harbour, owned by a cousin of mine. My father's nephew, he was about twenty. So Father arranged for him to take Mother into Halifax the day after Christmas. Father had a brother, a sea captain who lived in Halifax, and she was to stay there until she went to the hospital.

Halifax was a four or five hour drive then. It was all gravel roads, rutted and rough. You took the old car ferry across Halifax harbour.

So my cousin and Mother arrived at Uncle Sam's and she said, "Now, you take my suitcases up to the room and you better take me down to the hospital!" And I was born just after midnight on the twenty-seventh of December.

Well then, it snowed. There was two or three tremendously big snowstorms. Everything was tied up, including the train. It was buried outside of Dartmouth and nothing could move. Father was at home here with a houseful of little kids, wondering how he was going to get Mother and I home.

Captain Jeffrey Williams lived up across the bay here. He was captain of the only fisheries patrol boat on the east coast of Canada then. She was an old wooden ship, a coal burner, and he patrolled from Labrador down to the American border, on a monthly basis, pretty much year round. He happened to be in Halifax, I suppose, because of the holiday. Father got in touch with him to see if he could bring Mother and me home. Well, the old captain used to tell me the story very often. I would be in my thirties when he passed away.

He had Mother and I delivered to the dockside by a horse and sleigh. He went in with the chief engineer and gave Mother his cabin. We come out of Halifax in a southeast gale and a snowstorm and come down the coast. It was coming on dusk, dark, when he got to the outer fairway buoy, about eight miles off the coast. It was freezing up and the harbour, for about a mile, was froze up, a mile below the dock that he had to go to. "So," he used to tell me, "I made my decision."

He knew he hadda break ice and, of course, breaking ice with a wooden boat is pretty rough. He says, "I made my decision. I'll stay to sea all night then come in the next day, in the daylight." He says, "I went down to my cabin to tell your mother my decision."

I was only four pounds so I wasn't very big. He says, "I looked in my bunk and there was you, you little bugger. You're the smallest fella that ever changed my mind. When I took a look at you, I thought to myself, I haven't got it in my heart to keep a little fella like that out on the stormy sea all night. I'll have to go in!"

So he came in that night and he broke ice up here. Father could see him from here with the searchlights on. He broke ice up there to the wharf and we got in there ten o'clock. Father met us there with the horse and sleigh and brought us home.

That was my first sea trip. I was eight days old and four pounds soakin' wet. I always told my brothers and sisters they had the distinction of being born here in the old homestead but, by gad, I beat 'em all at goin' to sea!

One sort of oddity was my father. He was ten years younger then any of his siblings. My grandmother was fifty-two when my father was born. So he used to tell this story.

He went to school, like we all went, to a little one-room schoolhouse down the road here. Walked two miles to that. When he was twelve, he went on a vessel with Grandfather. When he was sixteen, they had quite a vessel here and they were hauling freight and fishing. They sailed from Halifax with a load of freight this day. As they come alongside the wharf, there was a gentleman on the dock and there was great greetings between Grandfather and this gentleman. Father was busy with the crew, getting the vessel tied up. Grandfather called to my father and said, "Archie! I suppose you don't know this gentleman?"

Father looked and he said, "No sir. He's a total stranger to me."

"Well," he said, "come on up on the wharf and meet your oldest brother!"

He was sixteen before he met his oldest brother! His oldest brother'd went to Boston and this was his first trip home after Father was born.

The last three of us, we were just a year apart. Three brothers. The youngest ones. We used to catch rabbits and, of course, we went to school. Often did the janitor work in the school.

We had a lot of cattle and sheep here that we looked after but in the late fall, after the middle of November, we would set rabbit snares, quite a ways away. There was lots of rabbits close here then, between here and the school, but we saved them 'til the snow got deep so we didn't have to travel too far.

Well, in the spring, we had a cat here. We always had two or three cats. Barn cats mostly but we always had one for a pet around the house. She was getting old and she had kittens and Father allowed us to keep one of the kittens. So we picked out this nice gray, sorta tawny and gray kitten and, oh, he was a real pet. We had him until about June or July and he disappeared.

Come the middle of November, we went off one Saturday morning. It was shortly after daylight and we had our chores done. We went down to the barrens, about a four or five mile walk. Took our hatchets and our snares and so on. There was lots of rabbits so we were setting snares all morning. It was kind of barren country with bunches of thick trees here and there. Old briar patches we used to call 'em. Peter Rabbit and the Briar Patch. Along about noontime, we spied a cat in one o' these briar patches. "By gosh, there's our kitten! He's grown some good though!"

We figured he was living in the wild somewhere and must have been feeding pretty good.

We surrounded the old briar patch and we eventually captured the cat and got him in a sack. He was nasty but we thought that was to be expected. He'd been in the woods all summer. My two brothers carried the sack and I carried the hatchets and gear and we struck off for home.

Well, we arrived home here about one o'clock. My mother was doing her baking and usual Saturday afternoon things. My father was laying in there on a couch, right under the window. He was an invalid then with multiple sclerosis. We marched in the house and announced to Mother that we had found our cat. And we let him outta the sack, here on the kitchen floor. The first daylight he saw, of course, was that window and he made a rush and he made a leap and landed up on the curtains over Father. Down come the curtains, curtain rods and the whole thing. Down on top of Father. I guess he was probably half asleep when this happened. He let a bellow out of him, "Get that damn cat outta here!"

The cat was scared and took off up the stairs. The door was open upstairs and he went in two rooms. Did the same thing. He just tried to go through the window and ripped the curtains down. What a mess he made!

Well, someone kept the door open and we rounded him up, chased him down the stairs and out. He went out through the door and, as he was going down the lane, we realized his tail was chopped off. It was only about this long. We had captured a bobcat and that's what we'd let loose in the house! When that happened I was probably about seven or eight.

We used to get in lots of little troubles. Going in swimming on the sly before we were supposed to. We used to start swimming here about the first weekend in June. Didn't matter how cold the water was, we would go anyway. Sometimes, that time o' year, we would accidently go in swimming and have our clothes on. Then we had to sneak up a ladder at the back of the house to get in our rooms. Someone would have to get up and get dry clothes and do a clothes change without Father and Mother knowing anything about it.

We used to run ice clumpers here around the shore, in the spring break up. You know, kids playing there, you get pretty bold. You jump on some pretty small ice cakes and see how long and how slow you could go and not get your feet wet. "Take Your Time! Take Your Time!" we chanted as you were going.

Doing this one day, one of my brothers had a brand new watch he'd got for Christmas. Pocket watch of course then. There was, "Take Your Time! Take Your Time!" And the first thing, the ice parted on him and down he went, right outta sight in the water. When he come back up, of course, his watch was full of salt water. I don't think it ticked afterwards. We tormented him for years about that. "Take Your Time! Take Your Time!"

33

The ghost story. It's quite a long story and it's connected with the story of my great-grandfather.

My great-grandfather built the old house, the first frame house, over there by the lighthouse. The family and neighbours always claimed there was a ghost in it. Well, Great-grandfather didn't like anyone talking about this ghost. But nobody knew who it was. And he was there when my grandfather built this place.

The old people died and they're buried over on an island, across the harbour from the lighthouse. There was an old Indian cemetery there and they were buried along side of that cemetery.

When they built the new lighthouse at the turn of the century, they tore the old house down. Of course, the ghost just transferred into the lighthouse and he's been there ever since.

Some odd things happened over there. When they put electricity in they had problems for years with keeping bulbs in the lighthouse. In fact, they still do. They even rewired it at one time. But I figure the old ghost, when we found out who it was, he had no electric lights in his day and he doesn't like them. He doesn't bother the upper light now, mind you, but the floor lights in the building are forever out.

There was a psychic here some years ago. She came as a guest when we first started the bed and breakfast. An old German lady and two of her nieces. One from Switzerland who didn't speak English at all and the other one knew sixteen languages and had a license to teach thirteen languages.

I caught on to her the first evening she was here. She was psychic. She asked me if there was a ghost in the lighthouse. I told her there was. When she wanted to know who it was, I couldn't tell her.

"Oh," she said, "that's unfortunate. But I'm so happy there's a ghost there because I've had several encounters with ghosts."

They were here for three or four days and she could tell your fortune. She told my life story better than I could remember it myself. In fact, she was so good at it, I was getting afraid that she knew some things I'd rather she didn't! And she did the same thing with my wife.

When she left, she took a handwriting sample of our son and sent us the analysis. The same thing. She told his whole life story from two lines of his handwriting. She wouldn't have known anymore about him had she lived here with him for twenty-five years.

Also, in the letter, she said, "I thought it was very important that you should know who the ghost is in the lighthouse. I made it my business to find out! It's the ghost of the great British admiral, Lord Horatio Nelson!"

Now the odd part of that was that she had seen nothing. There was nothing in the house at the time for her to read and we had told her nothing about the connection between my great-grandfather and Lord Nelson. When my great-grandfather was involved in the battle of Trafalgar and Nelson's body taken back to England for burial, Nelson was only forty-seven when he was killed and he'd been to sea most of his life. My great-grandfather was about twenty years younger. He was about twenty-seven then. I suppose Nelson decided, rather than go to London and be buried with that miserable body — it only had one eye and one arm anyway — he would stay aboard and sail with my great-grandfather. After all, he had been sailing with him for eighteen years. So he stayed with my great-grandfather for the rest of his career and then settled into the old house. I rather think sometimes, you know, that my great-grandfather knew who the ghost was and that's why he didn't want people talking about him. Because it was his revered old admiral and commanding officer for many years.

I think the two of them, Admiral Nelson in the lighthouse and Great-grandfather on the first island across the harbout there, come the dark nights, they still get together and have a little yarn. In fact, I put a picnic table out there on the hill for them!

He could be here as well as anywhere else!

People were here a couple of years ago from Saskatchewan. They'd been here at a convention and wanted to see a lighthouse. So they picked our place out of the tour book and stayed for a day or two. There was others here that night and I told quite a few stories, including the story of the ghost in the lighthouse.

Afterwards, we received this fellow's Christmas circular letter that he sent to his friends and relatives about what happened to them while they were here. Here's some of what he had said:

"After hearing the ghost story, which of course we believed and found amusing, it was time for bed. Myrna had left her small night bag in the rental car and went out to get it, alone. The ocean was extremely quiet and dark, the only light being that of an eerie beam, sending out its message from the top of the lighthouse, warning passing ships of the rocky dangers below. The darkness, the solitude and the mood could not have been better for what was about to happen.

"After getting her bag out of the trunk, Myrna closed the lid and started back for the house when the trunk popped open. Looking around, she thought it strange as she was sure it was latched. She shrugged and returned to slam it down. As she walked away a second time, the lid sprang open again sending a wave of goose-bumps up her arms and down her neck. She looked back at the car but saw nothing. She strained to look out into the dark but all was quiet and black. Slowly, she walked back and opened the trunk wide, looking inside. It was empty. There was absolutely no reason for the lid not to shut tight and latch. She slammed it down the third time and felt that it was firmly shut before starting back to the house.

"Before she had taken two steps, the lid popped open a third time! This time, she was feeling very nervous. She turned around quickly, shutting it hard and holding it down with her hand. She stood there, holding it for a few seconds, although it seemed much longer, to see that it was indeed closed this time. As she stood there alone looking around, she happened to gaze up towards the second story window and there she saw a glimpse of something she cannot forget.

"Through the dark glass of the old house, she could see an arm extended towards her, as though it was pointing at her. The cold wave of fear seemed to flood over her, freezing her to the spot. She strained to see the object clearer through the streaked old glass of the house. Instantly, she realized what was about to happen. The arm was raising and it seemed to be holding something in its hand. It was then she recognized it was the remote control unit that I was using to open the trunk of the new car every time she closed it!"

That probably stemmed from a little story I told them about some people who were here, oh, eight or ten years ago. They stayed here for about four days and then left on their way to Cape Breton. A day or two later I got a letter postmarked Sherbrooke Village. I thought, gosh, I don't know anyone in Sherbrooke.

I opened it and it was from these people that had just left a day or two before. They said a very strange thing happened. They'd left

36

here about ten in the morning for Liscombe Lodge and had dinner. On to Sherbrooke Village. Got there about two o'clock and parked their car. They went for a two-hour walking tour of the old village and when they returned, the trunk of the car was open. They had the only set of keys to the car in their pocket. They examined the trunk and there was nothing missing, nothing taken or anything. So they came to the conclusion that Nelson's ghost had hitched a ride in the trunk of their car, down to see some of his old friends in Sherbrooke, and they hoped that he would return with someone coming the other way.

I looked up the name and address of these people, in the register, and they were from out in Indiana. I waited about two weeks and I wrote a little note to them, telling them that there was no problem. That Nelson was back in residence in the lighthouse. So he got back with somebody!

There was an old gentleman, a distant cousin of mine, who never believed in ghosts, so he claimed. Years ago, there was a little cemetery down the road here where a lot of our folks are buried. It's a community cemetery and, back then, we used to look after it. In the fall, when the weather was windy, we'd pick a day that boats were tied up. Everyone would get together and we'd go down there working at the cemetery. Clean it up, you know.

Well, this day we were cleaning up the cemetery and this old gentleman was there, along with almost everyone else. He was quite a religious old feller and every once in a while someone would step on a grave and younger fellers, they'd say, "You'd better be careful or some feller's liable to reach up and grab ahold of you."

This old gentleman, he thought that was terrible. "Ah," he said. "There's no such a thing as ghosts! Your spirit goes to heaven when you die and that's it! There's nothing down there going to grab you."

So there was a lotta jostling around and joking all day and the work got done. Come supper time, the old lady next door to the cemetery invited this old gentleman for dinner that night. Supper. So he accepted.

Well, I had two brothers home here. They'd come home just after the war and they were fishing. They'd come in just the day before and they had a lot of huge, big codfish. Monstrous heads on them. And we took the notion.

We knew the old fella wouldn't be down there all that long 'cause he had cows to be milked and he had about a mile and a half to walk. So we rushed up home to the wharf and we speared up eight or ten of these great, huge fish heads. Now, in the fall of the year particularly, a cod head will glow in the dark. The eyes will glow right green. The bones, you can almost see the bone structure, right green in the night.

We stuck a bunch of these heads up on the highest tombstones in the graveyard and then we hid there.

It wasn't long. It was dark by five o'clock or so. After six o'clock we heard the old feller coming. It was a gravel road then and he had his rubber boots on so we could hear him scuffing along. He got up pretty near to the cemetery and he stopped. We heard him turn around and back he went. He went back to the house and he asked the lady if she had a light. He said it was so dark he was afraid he was going to walk off of the road. That's what he told her. Very few people had flashlights then but everyone had lanterns. She trimmed up a lantern and filled it with oil. Next thing, we saw him coming. As he got close to the cemetery, he started waving that lantern. And he kept *wa-a-ay* over the other side of the road, waving the lantern. And his feet started going faster and faster until he was on a dead run when he passed the cemetery. Well, we never did tell him what we'd done but we tormented him for a long time about not believing in ghosts. He'd seen those eyes in there looking out at him, he didn't know what it was! We had a laugh about it.

You know, listening to the old people tell stories was great entertainment for us young people in the winter, because there was no travelling here much. And back in those times, there was a ghost on every turn of the road and two or three in every cemetery. It was great entertainment to listen to the old people.

I remember one about my father and his cousin down the road here. They were just young fellas, going with two girls from East Jeddore, on the far side of the next harbour. Well, it was a five or six mile walk over there. Then, they'd borrow a boat from the old fishermen and go across the harbour.

So this Saturday night they went over. Now, half way through, there's a crossroad up here about two miles. It goes right along the head of the lake. And they always claimed there was a ghost at the head of the lake. So they went through there this Saturday evening, over to the east side of Jeddore.

I guess they probably went to church with the girls because a lot of the people over there at that time were Seventh Day Adventists. So they went to church and took the girls home, then they left to come home.

They rowed back across Jeddore harbour, hauled the boat up and secured it, and they started their five mile walk home. Coming through the crossroad, at the head of the lake, it was a beautiful moonlight night. Full moon. And Father took his watch out. They always wore pocket watches then, in their vest. Father took his watch out and he said to his cousin, "By gosh, Fred! It's just midnight and a full moon. We're just here in time to see the ghost at the head of the lake."

As soon as those words were out of his mouth, there was this blood curdling noise and the two of them took off so fast, the caps come offa their heads. And they didn't stop to pick 'em up! They ran the other mile through the woods, 'til they got over to the settlement, before they stopped. Then Father realized what it was they had heard. To this day, there's always a pair or two of loons nest in that lake and this is what hollered just as he mentioned about the ghost. It was a loon made her call. A mournful call in the night.

He wanted to go back then, when he realized what it was, and get the cap but no way. His cousin wouldn't go back. They went back the next morning after daylight and got their caps.

My wife, Mildred, was born in Canning, in the Annapolis Valley. She was the youngest of eight children. When she was three months old, her mother died and her father had all these children. It was Depression years and he was a carpenter. He had to move around quite a bit in order to get work and take work where he could get it. It was about impossible for him to do that with an infant child.

An old aunt looked after her for a bit but she was quite old and unable to do it anymore. So she was put out for adoption and she was adopted by a family in Halifax.

Now, her last name was Bennett. Spelt with two Ts. The people that adopted her were Bennets from England. English Bennets, spelt with one T. So they left her name the same and just dropped a T off it. She lived in Halifax 'til she was about four or five years old.

Then they moved out here to Musquodoboit Harbour. She had a very happy life. She had two adopted brothers. The people that brought her up were very nice people.

Some years after we were married, and Mildred knew that she was adopted, one of her sisters saw an announcement in the paper when our second daughter was born. "Born to Mr. and Mrs. Ivan Kent, nee Mildred Bennet, a daughter, Anne Elizabeth." Well, her brothers and sisters often wondered what ever became of their baby sister. Of course, adoptions were secret back then. No one could be told.

One of her sisters saw this announcement in the paper and two things gave her a clue. First, the name was the same, only spelt with one T on the Bennet. And the name that we called our daughter, Anne Elizabeth, was their mother's name backwards. Their mother's name was Elizabeth Anne. We didn't know that when we named our daughter. Anyway, that gave her another clue.

The sister was living in Truro. She went to the old sheriff, who was still living in King's County, who had handled the adoption. He was in his nineties. She asked him if that could be her sister and he said it very well could be.

So he gave her the address of the people who adopted her and she wrote to Mildred's father and mother. After they wrote a couple of letters back and forth, Mildred's adopted mother told her about it. They wrote then to Mildred and eventually we got to meet them all. In fact, they had a family reunion here, some years ago, of all the Bennett family. Very nice people. There's a couple of them have died since then. She still has two brothers and two sisters living.

So she wound up with, I guess in her two families, pretty near as many relatives as I had.

Now that was a funny thing. The psychic, the one that told us who the ghost was, when she read Mildred's palm, she studied her hand for about five minutes and then she sat down across the room and she told that whole story! She was so good at it. That's why I have pretty good faith in her that she's probably right about Nelson's ghost.

Halifax is our next stop — the old navy city with the beautiful harbour. I wonder if Nelson's ghost is stowed away in the trunk? It would be a good chance for him to visit some ghost-friends at one of the many graveyards. We'll take the bridge, the Angus L. Mac-Donald, across the harbour. It's a shorter route to the older, west-end street that is our destination. In an upstairs apartment we meet Ron DeMerchant.

Ron DeMerchant

I was born and brought up near a little place called Bath. It's in the upper end of Carleton County, about twenty miles south of Perth-Andover. About thirty miles north of Woodstock, New Brunswick. I was born in November of 1927.

When I was young and starting school, in my early years at school, we were in the middle of the depression of the '30s. The Dirty Thirties. No one really had anything. I grew up on a rather rundown old farm, which meant that we had the basic necessities. We could raise most of our own food, which meant that we did have enough to eat and a place to stay. I think it was probably better for us than for a lot of other people but there was no money available. You sold butter at ten cents a pound, eggs at ten cents a dozen. While you could do a lot more with ten cents then, than you can now, that still wouldn't get you very much.

There wasn't any organized sports or entertainment. Mostly, people gathered sometimes at one neighbour's house, sometimes another, to tell stories or sing or play a musical instrument, or something like that. You made your own entertainment. Ghost stories were pretty popular.

There was a lot of different versions of the Dungarvon Whooper. But the one that I heard, that was most popular, was that this young man just drifted into the Dungarvon River area, which happened a lot in those days.

He got a job in this lumber camp as a cook. Lumber camp life was hard and primitive. The work was hard; the wages were small and no amenities at all. So the main thing that the men could really feel that they had going for them was if they had a good cook. Well, this young man was apparently a very poor cook, according to the story. And, of course, not being many jobs available, you couldn't just pick up and go somewhere else and get another one.

So the men, instead of leaving and going somewhere else, they grumbled among themselves for awhile. Then they decided they'd get rid of the cook. Some of them, I don't know how many, made plans that they would kill the cook some night while he was asleep.

Apparently, while they were doing whatever they did to end his life, he woke up and started screaming. But he was too late. By the time he woke up, whatever damage was to be done had been done and he died a few minutes later. But, before he died, he did some screaming.

Well, I guess even now at certain times in that area, you can hear what's supposed to be this cook screaming, like he did before he died.

About twenty-five years ago, I was a patient in the hospital in Fredericton. I was in the same room with an elderly man, about the age then that I am now. Someone who was supposed to have been there told him this story.

They were up in the Dungarvon River country, working in a lumber camp in early March. Occasionally up there, in the late part of the winter, you'll get a day that you'd think was really spring. The sun will be out and the air will be nice and mild and the snow will be melting. This happened to be on a Sunday and the men weren't working so they were out in the camp yard. From down in the woods, they heard somebody hollering. They thought someone from another camp went for a walk or something and got lost in the woods. So they answered it. Each time it would holler, they would holler. Each time they would hear it, it would be closer to them.

Finally, the hollering or screaming was coming from right in among the group. But they couldn't see anyone. They could hear this coming from right in among them yet they couldn't see anything at all. And there were no tracks in the snow.

Apparently, the Dungarvon Whooper.

This one's kind of funny. There was a lumber camp near Juniper, New Brunswick, where the Flemming Company had a big operation a few years back. Men would go to Juniper and hire on there at head office, then they'd be sent to different camps up in the woods.

At one of these camps, years and years ago, there had been a drifter who got a job in the woods with the company. At that time, they pretty well closed the camp down for a few days at Christmas, so that the men who had families could go home. Usually, they'd try to get someone who didn't have anyone or any place to go, to stay and look after the camp and any horses that were left there that they didn't take out with them. This drifter said he had no place to go and nothing really to do so he'd stay.

While the other men were gone, there came a big snow storm. It was a few days later than they had intended before they got back. They found him on one of the bunks, dead. Apparently been dead for a day or two. The story went that that camp was haunted after that. They didn't use the camp again, so the story goes, but that may have just been because they had cut all the lumber within easy reach. Just moved to another site nearer to more lumber. I don't know.

I heard an old gentleman, who was a pretty good storyteller, tell one time that he had been up there. The job was finished and he was walking back out on his way down to Juniper, hoping to catch a ride home. He was really tired and, as he walked by this old camp, which was still standing, he decided he'd go in and rest for awhile. Maybe stay overnight and walk out the next day.

He said, "I was tired and it was starting to come dark. I looked at the old camp and I said, I'm going in." He said, "I went in and I set down on the old bunk and I unlaced my boots. And pretty soon, this fella was sitting on the bunk, right beside me.

"He said, 'Well, there's just two of us here.'

"And I said, 'By the old Christ, there's only gonna be one of us here as soon as I get my rubbers laced up!'

The old fella said, "I started down the road, running as hard as I could. And I ran and ran and I got so out of breath that I tripped

43

and fell down. I was so out of breath, I couldn't get up. I'm lying there, just gasping for breath. Looked up and this fella was sitting on a stump, right beside the road.

"He said, 'Well, that was quite a little run we had.'

"I said, 'By the old Christ, that ain't nothin' to the one we're gonna have soon's I get my breath back!'"

I experienced this myself. Now I don't know what it was, imagination or what, but there was a road around Bath.

In the days when most people travelled with horses, they used it quite a bit because it was a shortcut to get from one main road to another. After cars come in, it fell into disuse. Occasionally, someone would drive through there.

I remember that, if I came through there all alone in the car late at night, at a certain spot I would get this feeling that there was someone in the car with me. Same as if you were in a room alone and someone comes in and you don't see or hear them. Just get a feeling that there's someone there. I'd have this feeling so strong that, without thinking what I was doing, I'd look over to speak to somebody and then realize I'm all alone in the car. But it would be this really strong feeling.

I didn't say anything about it to anyone because I thought they'd say, "Oh, you're imagining things."

But one day, I did mention it to a friend of mine. He said, "Well, you're not the only one. It happened even a little stronger with me. One night I was coming through there and I got this feeling that there was someone with me. I looked over and there was a man sitting on the passenger seat beside me. Even though I knew I was all alone in the car. There was no sense of anybody moving or anything when he came there. He just was there.

"I spoke to him. No answer. I put my hand over to touch him but there was nothing there that you could touch. And yet I could see him, as plain as I ever saw anything, sitting on that seat beside me!

"I was kind of nervous and I gave him a pretty merry ride through there. Just at a certain spot, he just disappeared! There was no sense of anybody moving when he went. One second he was there and the next second he was gone."

Whether this really happened to him, or he was just elaborating on my story, I don't know. But I do know that I would get this really strong feeling of somebody being in the car with me.

Away back when my father was a young man, probably nineteen or twenty, a fella that was a close friend of his was going around with this girl. I guess quite seriously. In the fall, he left to go to work at a lumber camp for the winter. When he came back in the spring, this girl had taken up with another fellow.

My father said his friend wasn't a bad sort of a fellow but, especially if he happened to be drinking a little bit, he could do some pretty irresponsible things. Anyway, he threatened this guy to stay away from her.

One night her new guy was at the girl's house and the fellow she had been going around with went to the place with his rifle.

Father always said that he thought his friend just intended to scare him. But they were sitting in the kitchen and he fired through the closed door. The bullet went in through the door and struck her. Killed her.

This happened in March, I believe. Justice was pretty swift and sure in those days. This was in 1904. He was arrested and put on trial and found guilty. He was hanged in July, about four months after he had shot her.

It was about thirty miles from where he lived to Woodstock, which was where he was held and where he was to be hanged. He wanted my father to go and get his body and bring it out to his parents' home. He was to be hanged on a certain date, right after midnight.

My father went to Woodstock with his team of horses and he went in the jail and talked to the fel la for awhile. Dad said he didn't seem a bit concerned or anything. Just as calm as if they had just met somewhere and were sitting talking. When it came time for Father to leave, they stood up and shook hands. And this fella said, "I'm coming back to see you afterwards."

Well, that night, or in the small hours of the morning, as soon as they would release the body, they put it in a casket and my father started home with it. He had a fairly fast road team and got to this young man's parents' place at just about the darkest hour of the night. Just before dawn started to break. He left him there and went home.

45

He unhitched his team from the express wagon. When the horses got to the stable door, and he never saw them do that before, instead of going in they'd go up to the door and then run backwards. Away from the door. They did that four or five times. He talked to them and coaxed them and, after awhile, he got them in. But they just tramped and snorted for quite a few minutes. Finally they settled down and started to eat. He went to the house and went to bed.

He always said afterward, he wished he had thought to say this fella's name and see if the fella would speak to him or anything. Because he never saw those horses act that way before nor since.

You know, it's been a long time since I met many of the people in this book, yet in my mind I can still see their faces and I can still hear their voices every time I read these pages. One of the kindest faces and warmest voices belongs to the man you'll meet next. His name is Aubrey Whiley and he lives just outside of Halifax in a community called Hammonds Plains. When Aubrey was a young boy, back in the early 1900s, it was a busy community.

Aubrey Whiley

That was my father's sawmill business and I took it on after he passed away. So I kept building the barrels and I worked with my brothers to build it up to where it is now. But the barrel business began to ease out so we had to turn to boxes. We turned our mill over to making fish boxes of all types.

I was raised right up here at Hammonds Plains. I worked with my father, a young boy at the age of eight or nine, going around the mill after school and doing a little work. Carry out the slabs and one thing and another. So I growed right up here in the business. It was hard work but Dad, he didn't rush us anymore than what we could do. He give us a time to do it. It was rugged work but we got used to it. It didn't bother us.

Sunday, we hadda be in church. My dad was a church man. He was a choir singer. And the children had to be there. So we followed right along in his footsteps. We was dressed up, looking pretty sharp for Sunday. We went along with that. Then this accident come on him and he got killed in the mill. He died there accidentally. Drowning. When that happened, it shocked everybody. I was

47

shocked. Didn't know where to turn. I thought, "Well, I have to take over where he left off."

Taking over, there just was my mother and me. I didn't have a wife. I didn't have somebody that I could talk to. So I went out seeking a wife. I went out looking.

I went to the dance hall. There's gonna be a lotta girls around that dance hall. I never danced in my life but I had to learn, to get acquainted with somebody. So I got on this floor and I got dancing. I was stepping on these girls' toes saying, "Excuse me. I'm not quite accustomed to what's going on but I think I can learn."

So I danced with a girl. When another dance'd come up, I'd find another girl. I was shopping for to find a wife, really, but I was dancing along to find her.

I was about twenty-five or so, and I was going along dancing and we had a talk with some of the girls there. They was dressed well, you know. This girl that I was thinking about she was dressed so highly. Oh my. So I said to her, "Where do you live?" I had a car then, way back in them days.

She said, "I don't live too far from here, in Halifax."

So I drove her home and she asked me to come in. I went in her house and sat down and she offered me a drink. I think it was coffee or tea. We sat around. But this girl had so much clothes. So I said, "Now I'd like to see your wardrobe. I'm not inquisitive but, by God, the way you're dressed." I looked in this wardrobe and I see all of these clothes hanging up. I said to myself, "You can't be the wife for me because I couldn't afford to buy the clothes that you got!"

I was joking around and I said, "If you marry a man, would you want to extend your clothes or just say I got enough to last me through?"

"Oh no,"she said. "I would have to have something different. I would like to change and follow the stars."

I said, "That's nice."

Anyway, she gave me a kiss and I said goodnight. I didn't think I'd be back there anymore because her way of living was gonna be higher than what I got coming in from my father's business. So I thought, "I'll look around for somebody else."

The next time, I went to the church. Where the young people was all there in the church and they all was singing. I was a pretty good singer so I was singing pretty strong, you know. Some of these girls began to look at me. I thought, "Maybe they might come over and shake hands with me after the service." And they actually did!

I didn't go anywhere for a week or two. I just stayed around home. On the Sundays I went to my church. Then come to me that it was a girl up in Hammonds Plains, right in here. A girl right across the road. She was much younger than I was. I was twenty-five or twenty-six. She was about ten years younger. Her mother used to make a beautiful gingerbread. She had it out on the front step there and I got the aroma across the road. I loved gingerbread so, after supper, I went over and I said, "I smelled something this afternoon."

"Oh," she said, "I did have a gingerbread."

I said, "Who made it?"

She said, "My daughter."

I said, "You have a daughter?" I knew she had a daughter all the time. "I'd like to talk to her. I might be able to get her to make me a gingerbread someday." Joking like that.

Anyway, the girl come out. Just the same like the woman I'm married to now. I said, "You're too young to cook like that."

"Oh," she said, "Mama gave me some instruction. Would you care for a piece?"

I said, "I would."

So I sat down. She had a glass of milk and this gingerbread she brought to me. Oh my. We had a long talk and, that gingerbread, I'm telling you!

That night I begin to think. "If I can find a woman that makes her gingerbread like that!"

I knew people were gonna think that I'm marrying too young a girl if I get in with a girl that young. Anyway, it went on. I give it two or three weeks. I slowed down a little to get myself together. Then I went over. We talked and talked. Then we went for a little drive in the car. We drove around, talking.

I said, "I'd like to have you for a friend of mine. A girlfriend. I believe I'd choose you for a friend if you would accept."

She said, "Well, I'll have to consider."

I said, "You got a few days to do that. I'll take my time."

So, after a couple of days' time, she come back and she said, "Yes."

We were going around together, oh, four or five months. I decided that I would rush a little, into marriage. I said, "Would you marry me, you think?"

She said, "That's another big step to make. That's something I'll have to take back and consider awhile."

By God, about a month or so after that, she made up her mind that we could. We never set an engagement or anything. We just went along knowing that I was looking forward to what I said to her. And be blessed if we didn't come up in October. My father died in April. In October, we was married.

She was young but she was a very good worker. A good cook and a good housekeeper. I was saying to myself, "I don't think I want too many children 'til we get organized, you know. For a few years."

But, be blessed, our family was coming faster than I expected. We had a boy. I said, "Well, he'll grow up and someday might be a help to me."

Then the next one was a girl. The wife said, "A girl and a boy. That's it. We'll stop at that."

But that wasn't all. That was only the beginning. When we ended up, we had eight children. Three girls and five boys. I don't know how the good Lord worked but we raised those children. They all growed up.

One daughter went to Arizona and she married a minister. I didn't know the man but a wonderful man she married. I never went to the wedding. It was too far for me. The next year, I think, they come here and visit us. What a fine man he is.

The other daughter went out to live with her aunt in the Winnipeg area. She got married to a fella that was in the service. So my daughters got two fine men. I'm proud of them.

The boys, my sons, they married local girls. They're lucky. They've got two fine girls they married. One got twins, the other one got two children. They work here with me but we all get along together. We don't have a problem with life, so far.

After we got married, I lost my dad's mill. That was a water-powered mill, way back there. That mill burnt down one night. I didn't know anything about it. We went back the next morning with the horse and wagon, the mill was flat. I didn't know where to turn. When the men got there, I told them there was no work today, our mill burnt down.

I didn't know what to do. I went to work for awhile — construction, on the highway.

Then we come out here and we built a mill. Put in electricity this time. Had it all ready to saw and, that night, that mill burnt down! Never saw one piece of lumber in that mill! I said, "Oh, I'm finished. I'm to the end of my journey."

I give up, pretty well. I didn't know what I could do. So I went looking for a job. I went to the shipyards, to the dockyards, the public service, all these places. I filled in applications, all were turned down.

I said to my wife, "I don't know what I'll turn to."

So a man up the road here had a mill. I went to talk to him and I said, "I heard you had a mill for sale."

He say, "Yes. You want to buy it?" Great friend of mine, you know.

I said, "Yes, I want to look at it." But I didn't have any money to buy anything.

So I went up to look at it. I didn't know whether I wanted it or not. I was discouraged.

He called me the next night asking, "What about that mill?"

I said, "I'm trying to get my mind together but I haven't made up my mind what I can do."

I laid back a few days. That man called me four times. And me with no money!

So I went up and I talked to him. I said, "I don't have any money. What do you want for that mill?" A big mill. Sixty-five feet long and forty feet wide. It wasn't built no more than ten or eleven years before that.

He said, "$125. $125 will give me a new life."

I said," I'll tear that mill down, move it and rebuild it."

My son was in Montreal then. I had no help, only the younger fella here. So I took my son and another little fella. They was about eleven or twelve years old. They was going to school. This was in June. I bought myself a new shovel to rip all these shingles and stuff off the roof. I got up on that roof and I couldn't see no end to it at all. I thought, "What is one man gonna do up on here?"

I kept my head down and didn't look at the roof. I looked at my work. Boys, I had this new pointed shovel and I was ripping them shingles off. And I could work then. I was just rolling that tar paper off that roof and everything.

Then I started taking the boards off with my ripping bar. I said, "Now, you fellas draw the nails out and pile the boards up on the truck." I had a half-ton truck. The boys was working. I was working.

I took that mill down in about a week and a half. In two weeks, I had that big mill tore down and hauled that lumber down here. The rafters, I couldn't haul in the half-ton. They were about twenty-five feet long. I had to haul them down on a horse and wagon.

And the sills underneath the bottom of the mill was ten by ten. Boys oh boys. No help. Only these little boys to help me to move them off the mill and get them out to the road so I could put them on the truck or the wagon. I said, "Boys, you get on each end and I'll get in the middle and you'll help me."

But I was so much taller than them, the boys were bearing down more then they were lifting! I said, "Boys, I think you better let go. I'll take over."

And I carried this stuff up to the road. I don't know, really, where I got the strength. I did ruin my back. I went down to the doctor. The doctor said, "You must have been lifting tractors! You're all strained up."

I said, "I was lifting something pretty near as heavy."

However, we built that mill up in October. We had the same mill we got out there running. I walked through that mill, tears come to my eyes. I couldn't believe myself. I had it built, that mill, in eleven days.

I was so proud of it. I didn't think that really could happen. I know that the good Lord was the only one that opened the way for me to get this job done.

The oldest boy was in Montreal. He always loved a mill. I never even told him that I had a new mill. Some of the boys went up there and told him.

He wants to see this mill so he comes down. And, by God, the next morning he was working in the mill.

I said, "God, you come down on vacation and you're working hard as I am." I needed the help.

Then his two weeks was up. I said, "Well, son, I hate to lose you but I wouldn't want you to leave a good job to depend on me. I don't know where I'm at. I don't have enough to pay you what I should be paying you. I'm glad you was here. I enjoyed your help and I'm sorry you gotta go back, but I know you have to go back."

He said, "No, Dad. I think I'm gonna stay with you."

I said, "That's good but I'll have to explain some things to you. I can't pay you the ordinary wages like these other people. We been burnt out. We don't have the money."

He said, "I'll go along with what you can pay me. I hope it won't always be that way."

I said, "I hope it won't either."

By God, he's still here today! I know the good Lord has led me. He blessed me and He's kept me this far.

Back in the horse and wagon days, that was rugged. Rugged but it was nice. It wasn't much harder than the work we do around here but it was a longer day. You know, you leave here six o'clock or quarter to six and it'd take four hours to get to Halifax driving a team with a load of barrels on. You'd take that load off, another four hours to come back. A couple hours in Halifax. We'd take around forty-five fish barrels. Fish barrels are much heavier than the apple barrels. Fish barrels had to be water-tight, you know, to hold pickled fish. They used to send it to the West Indies. They couldn't send nothing down there fresh so they had to salt it.

I had one experience that I don't think I'd want to go back there again. My dad sent me in, when I was a little boy, to take this load into town. I said, "Dad, I don't know anything about town."

He said, "Oh, the horse knows about that. Horse knows where he's going. Just let the reins slack on the horse. He'll take you."

That night I never sleep one wink.

I got up in the morning, fed the horse, hitched the horse in, started for Halifax. I went down through the Kearney Road and right into Halifax. I get to Halifax, I didn't know one street from another. Went right down Robie Street. Around the Commons. That horse, he went right down Morris Street, right down to Water Street. I was taking the barrels to A.M. Smith, a big merchant. Horse went straight onto their wharf and I thought, "Isn't this something!"

I went in the office and I said, "I'm Whiley."

"Oh yes, I know your father. You got fish barrels."

I say, "Yeah. I have a load of barrels on."

So I back into the warehouse, took the barrels off and I get a slip for the barrels. I never got paid for them. And I said, "Back home."

But the horse got to have his dinner. I got to have mine.

By gosh, when he came to Grafton Street, he turned on Grafton and stopped. I looked and I see that was the forge where we used to stop. He stopped right there in front of that forge. I took him outta the wagon and take him in there. I say, "I'm Whiley."

He say, "Okay," the man that owned the forge there. I put the horse in the stall and then feed him and I paid for his feed. I went and got my dinner. When I come back all was on my mind was, Dad said leave them reins slack.

So I was setting up on this wagon, still nervous. He come up from Grafton Street, come up Jacob hill. We went up on Gottingen Street there and we got up on Creighton Street and by God, when I looked, we was back on Robie Street. That's where I come in at. That horse must be on the right route. And that's the first time I settled down from the time that Dad told me I was going to town, until that horse's head was veered for home.

A load of barrels would be worth around about $35, $40. You only got seventy-five cents apiece for them.

We had a pair of oxen. I remember I took these oxen down in the Bay, one of them, one night. The fella couldn't shoe him until late so we come back, by gosh, about ten or eleven o'clock. It was dark. Pitch dark. I was driving this ox back from the Bay after I had him shod and I was whistling because, my God, I was nervous. I was whistling to keep everything a little away from me. And this ox stopped in the middle of the road! I thought maybe his feet was hurting him. His shoes or something. He stopped and he wouldn't go. "Go on," I said. "We're going home."

But it was some kind of object or something that he smelled on the road there. On each side o' the road. Anyway, I went up along side of the head. I coaxed him. He was pretty good. He started walking slow. He went over to that side the road and he went along. Then it seemed like there must be something on the other side o' the road. He went back on this side and we got past. But when he got past, that ox took off. All I had was a chance to reach down and I grabbed the tail. I said, "Onliest way you leavin' me is if this tail leave you!" Boys, we took off there! You talk about going! Anyway, we got home that night.

One time, we had, down in the county road, a place called Kearney Brook where we used to water the horses. Dad said, "Don't let the horse go down in that brook because he could upset the wagon." This load o' barrels was high you know. Musta been pretty near ten or twelve feet high when they were piled up on the wagon. So I was driving the horse and I'd come from a picnic and I fell asleep on the front of the wagon. The horse went down in the brook and this thing rocked and I woke up. By gosh, the wagon was very near getting ready to upset in the brook. Well, looka here, I was never so scared in my life. The horse went in there for water because he was thirsty. But we had a bucket on the side of the wagon to water him. Flat load you could drive down in there. Anyway, I got one hand on the side of the rack and driving him with one hand, I got him out on the road again.

Well, there was no more sleep got in my eyes on that day.

Hammonds Plains was, one time, a place that was self-employed. All the people here, that lived in this place, they all worked for each other. Making the hoops for the barrels. In the woods. Some would be in the mills. Some would be cooping in the cooper shop. This was an industrial place. You come in here you could hear the shop where they make barrels. Pounding on these barrels. They was a people that had a trade. They must have brought it here with them.

They could make a barrel from the tree. My father showed me the tools they used. Not mill work, but take the tree and split that wood out and make a watertight barrel.

Back in them days life was right. Somebody asked me if I'd wanta go back? I said, "Well, I look back and talk back but, for to go back, I don't think I could handle it."

I haven't often gathered stories or poetry from family or in-laws. However, I'm glad I did get together with Jessie Ellis. His son, Alan, is married to my sister, Mona. Jessie has since passed away but his wife, Thelma, still lives in the old family home at Port Maitland, Nova Scotia. That's just a few miles up the shore from Yarmouth.

Jessie Ellis

The Ellises were fishermen and mill owners. I think most of the settlers in the area here were English descent. My grandfather was the owner of a store and a lobster factory in Cape St. Mary's. He operated that business in the summertime. In the wintertime, he moved his family down to Wellington, which was about half way from Port Maitland and Yarmouth. It was a summer business as far as he was concerned. He died very shortly before I was born. That was in 1913.

My father, Harvey Ellis, worked in the lobster factory with his father. They operated a small vessel. A sixty-foot schooner, I suppose. A two master, the *Old Defender*. They used to go on voyages as far as Halifax for supplies for the lobster cannery, buying cans and coal. It was operated by him and his brother Stanley.

One of my earliest recollections is the first trip I ever went with them. Summer business then was night fishing. The large schools of herring came into the bay here and the local fishermen'd go out there in the night and chase the whales around to find the herring schools. Then they would probably wind up catching a boat-load of fish. Coming home in the morning, I was sitting down looking around at the water. My uncle grabbed me by the shoulder and said, "Now you look right over the stern. You're gonna see something!"

The thing that I saw was a large whale that just propelled himself right out of the water, practically full length, and then fell back with a monstrous splash! It was quite a sight for any little boy. I was ten or twelve years old.

I had a line of my own that I was supposed to look after. That was the extent of my business at that time.

I remember another time there came up a terrific thunder storm. We just weren't able to do anything. It rained so hard that you couldn't see anything on the water to find any herring or any fish. So we just had to fool around there until it stopped. We got our trip of fish after the thunder and lightning moved away. Then, when we got home in the morning, we found that the largest stable, E.H. Porter's Livery Stable, had burned down during that thunder storm. Hit by lightning. So there was some great excitement around Port Maitland that night while we were still out on the water.

We did a lot of the usual things that children do. We swam and we played ball. I can remember, lots of times too, we sneaked down to the shore after the old fellas hauled their lobster traps and dories in and gone home. We borrowed their dories and went out back of the wharf, in the surf, to have a lot of fun rowing back and forth in the breakers, little seas that came in on the beach, you know. I suppose we learned a certain amount of seamanship at the oars, at that time.

We'd go down there and borrow those dories without any permission at all. Never asked a soul and nobody ever said a word. Of course, we didn't damage them in any way but I still thought it was, for some of the characters that were around there, a little strange that they didn't have a few words to say.

There were a couple of old fellas I remember real well who were around when I was just a youngster. They had some herring nets out near the beach that they were gonna go haul. They had a good catch of herring but, after they got their dories pretty well filled, one of them said to the other, "We're getting quite heavy."

The other fella said, "Well, I can swim just as far as you can!"

So they kept right on picking herring. By and by, down went the dories and they did swim ashore. And that was roughly a third of a mile, in salt water. They were really tough old boys.

Cars came into Port Maitland in my younger years but there weren't very many. Our local stable proprietor finally got himself a truck. On Saturday night, he would gather up everybody that wanted to go to town and take them down in that. In fact, there were two trucks. Carried people down so they could go to the picture show, to the movies. A pretty big deal at that time. Provided recreation for a lot of people. It was quite a few years before enough of us got cars so we took to going in ourselves.

When I was fishing with my father, we went out the morning of the sixteenth of April. It was quite fine, before daylight, when we went out. As the forenoon went along, the sea began to build up. And since it was a high water in the morning, had we gone when it was time to go, we could have got back in. But times weren't all that great. Father of course wanted to get all he could out of the day, so he decided he was gonna stay. We could only see two or three boats but they stayed, so we stayed. By the time we began to lift traps it was extremely rough. Seas probably, at the time, were building up to about twenty feet. It was a real tough day.

We decided to go home and when we got in there, the whole inshore fleet was in there too. So there'd be about forty boats gathered there all together. As long as the tide was down, it was fine. But as the tide began to come up and got up to top height, it started to come over the wharf. So things got tough quite fast. One or two of the fellas got washed right off of the wharf into the boats. To make matters worse, there was a fish trap here at the time. They had started to put out their poles, those big fifty foot poles.

Anyway, we got tied up to the wharf and some of the fellas got their heads together and they said we got to do something. They took off in a car to see some of the farmers around the back country. First thing we knew, oxen began to arrive on the beach.

What they did was tie four yoke of oxen together, in spans, then hook the whole bunch together on a big chain, then drive a boat up on the beach and hook that chain around the boat. A friend and I stayed in the water and put rollers underneath the boats. The minute they landed, they hooked this big chain up in the bow of the boat, hooked all those oxen on, and started off. One of my greatest regrets is the fact that we couldn't have had a tape recorder there at the time, to hear the noise and the things that went on. Because you know very well that most of those teams weren't just depending on gee and haw. They had some spirits inside of 'em to help things along. There were some real fancy noises going on there.

All the boats wound up on the beach and everybody was saved. That was one of the real experiences of my fishing career. If I remember correctly, I think there were twenty yoke of oxen that walked out there, from the various farms around the back country, to help the fishermen out that night. It was a real big deal that, when you stop to think, most of those cattle had never been around that place in the night. To think that they were able to do it was really something.

One of the things we looked forward to, to make things more interesting at nights when we went out fishing, was that these whales were more or less predictable. They arrived with the herring schools and the same ones would be back. Remember, this was at night; you couldn't see them. It was remarkable that those things could navigate around a fleet. Lots of times there'd be about a hundred boats. Those whales would go around and get their herring amongst all those nets and very seldom ever get tangled.

There was one or two times we'd have a school of herring under our lights, underneath the boat. The whales would look around everywhere for herring and, finally, they'd decide that we had 'em all. Then they'd come and get 'em. Kind of make your hair stand up, because the whale would come and circle right around the boat, look things all over, then he'd go off to one side and make one great, big rush right underneath that boat. The water would all turn white and bubbles would keep rushing up. You could actually hear the bubbles exploding after that beast had gone underneath the boat. Took all our fishing lines and never touched the net. Not one of them ever got fouled up in the net at all.

I remember one morning, we fished all night and we had quite a lot of herring in our net. Some of the fellas would make a business of going to town. They'd take the herring along with them. So they came along, and we had three quarters of a net full.

"You fellas come pick these herring?"

"Sure." So they came and took the net aboard their boat and started in to work. And I noticed a big whale working off towards them, sort of fooling around. He didn't appear to be in a hurry to go. When it got about fifty or sixty feet away it disappeared. I knew very well the next time, it was gonna come up so close somebody was gonna get scared. And sure enough it did. It come along and blew about fifteen feet from the boat. These two fellas that were picking herring were back to at the time. They almost jumped overboard. It was funny.

There was one whale had a peculiar sound to its blow. We never, ever got to see that one but it had an obstruction in its blowhole that would lift as he blew. "Blub, blub, blub, blub." You know, about like a locomotive with its stack half off is what it sounded like.

And depending on how long he stayed under water and when he come up, affected what it would sound like when he finally blew. Some of those times it was really funny. We always knew that one just as soon as he'd show up. He came back for a good number of years.

There have been some shipwrecks through the years. Old Trinity Ledge out here has not been a kindly place for a lot of ships.

A large coasting vessel went up on Trinity, called the *Happy Home*. It's one of the ones that we remember real well because the fishermen in the village were some of the first to reach the ship. They had a big hand in removing the crew and bringing them in safe. The captain of the ship was so pleased with the way things went that he donated the ship's bell to the school. At the time of the original schoolhouse, it was on the outside and summoned all the children to classes. Since this new school was built, they've taken it from the outside and put it in the library. So it's still there to this day.

The last ship that went there was the only one that I had anything to do with. The word came from the Yarmouth radio station that the ship had hit the ledge. The crew had sent out a mayday and wanted some help. So half a dozen boats or more of us started off. When we got out there, we found them in their lifeboat. The ship had gone down. Punched a big hole in the bottom of it. There were three women on it. It started to go up to St. Mary's Bay after a load of pulpwood, I guess. After it bounced off of Trinity Ledge, why, it didn't get very far. I guess I was one of the first boats there but I didn't have any part in bringing the people ashore. One of the other boats took them aboard. Had a bigger, newer boat than I did and was able to give them more comfort.

The other shipwreck there that I remember happened in the year after I was born. I was only a year old. It was a Royal Mail steam packet, a big iron steamer that went from England to Saint John and carried the trans-Atlantic mail. It was a real deal because it was on the ledge a long time. It took a long while to disintegrate.

It was also a mob scene too because the fishermen were able to get aboard it. In all kinds of boats. Some of them, naturally, they had their eyes on different items. It had a large liquor cargo. It had just recently been refurbished and had all the bedsheets and things for the passengers. Brand new. To this day I imagine, here around Port Maitland, you could dig out some of those sheets and things that were removed from that wreck.

My father and his brother decided they'd like to have the piano to take home. They put it up on deck and had gone back for something else. When they come back, the piano'd disappeared and there was I don't know how many cases of rum piled in the same place the piano had been!

From the Ellis homestead, let's give ourselves a treat and take the Digby to Saint John ferry towards our next destination, Grand Manan Island. Then we rent a car and drive to Blacks Harbour, New Brunswick, just in time to catch another ferry. Once on Grand Manan, it's a short drive to Annie Foote's home at Seal Cove. I talked with Annie late in 1998, on the phone, and she told me she was now being asked to meet with tourists and tell them some of the history of Grand Manan. I can just bet she includes a good story or two from her own experiences.

Annie Foote

When I was twelve, I started in writing about my baby sister who was born. I'm twelve years older than she. In the first verse, I forgot all about my baby sister. I wrote about Wood Island and its summertime. Then, at the last, I thought, "Gee, this doesn't say much about Leona!" So I closed it with mentioning her again.

But it is what we did on Wood Island, pretty much. And I wrote . . .

Through the fog the sun doth shine
Wreathing you in halo, baby sister mine.
It's Wood Island and it's summertime.

Though to me you're not less dear
When the day, with sunshine, is bright and clear.
Summer with its endless hours
Full of birds and bees and flowers.

There are days of going haying
And there are days of just plain playing
As round the shores and woods we tramped
To build sand castles or a camp.

With sky so blue we can see beyond,
Gazing at its reflection in Big Pond.
It's a time when fur bearers have less hair
And birds shed feathers everywhere.

It's the time when insects zoom
And fruit has ripened from springtime's bloom.
It's a time for fishing and that's not all.
It's a time for watching and playing ball.

It's time to watch the fleecy lamb
Taking nourishment from its dam.
It's a time of warmth, a time of clover,
A time of feeling good all over.
It's dulsing time and time to swing,
To walk on stilts, to hear cowbells ring.

We celebrate in a very special way
When summer brings us Dominion Day.
With picnics and ball and games galore
Which we participate in though our tummies are sore.

It's a day for cheering and a day of yelling
And a day for eating watermelon.
And there's time for silences, so dear to the soul,
As we lie curled up at the old tree's bole.

But summer brings something better than that.
A dozen kids, or so, in the old sand rack
Reached after swimming with porpoise,
        three-quarters of a mile or so.
They nudge you, they budge you, they whistle, they blow.

There is so much to do and that is the reason
That summertime is a wonderful, beautiful season.
The birds all burst into song to greet it
And all who love summer, at daybreak, will meet it.

Will feel the warmth of the day, will respond to the mood
And will plunge in the ocean but not in the nude.
Though the water is icy, the water can't chill
The children for whom the sun doth stand still.

Summer's a time when sandpipers flock
To gather with children, to skip from rock to rock.
Summer's a time to pick penny royal and all herbs Gram uses.
There even is one that soothes our stone bruises.

Late in the summer we mustn't lag
In picking Indian hemp and digging roots of sweet flag.
Oh summer! We love you! Love you we must!
You give us so many hours twixt daylight and dusk.

About summer, parents have a curious thought.
They think it is sweet but they think it is short.
And that is the reason, or so they say,
That they give us freedom to work or to play.

This isn't really a silly old rhyme.
It's a thank you to God for the summertime.
A summertime made much sweeter this year
By the birth of baby sister who, in May, did appear.

My mother played the organ in the church and we went to church, if we behaved ourselves. Everyone went. It was really fun.

I remember the first time I went. I went to see the devil! I probably was about four years old and I knew that the church was God's house. I had probably been to Sunday School before then but anyway, I asked Dad, "Does the devil have a house?"

He said, "It's one and the same. You keep your eyes open and you'll see him."

So it's like the little girl who wished to see the devil and she did. I wished to see him and when he rose up, up in the choir, I said, "There's the devil! There's the devil!"

She had a beautiful velvet, black hat on with a red rose on it. I'd never seen her before. She didn't look very fiendish. I don't know, it was just someone I didn't know.

We sat with Uncle Eugene so Mum could keep an eye on us, I suppose. He used to go down in the church cellar and put wood in the furnace, and this type of thing, before the service.

One time we just made up our minds that every time "redeemed" was said, we'd say "Eugene."

So they sang the hymn.

> Redeemed, how I love to proclaim it.
> Redeemed by the blood of the Lamb.

Anyway, the chorus goes, we sang,

> Eugene, Eugene. Eugene, Eugene.
> His child and forever I am.

And he said, "Mmmmmm, mmmmm." He was a great old character.

One time there was a boy. Well, there's a hymn, "I'm Going Through. Jesus, I'm going through." But he sang:

> I buckled on my skates. The ice was buckling too.
> I hung my head and cried, Oh God, I'm going through.
> I'm going through. Jesus I'm going through.
> I cannot swim a stroke. Oh God, what will I do?

We had lovely Sunday School teachers and I think all the Bible that I ever learned, I learned in Sunday School. One teacher, Lila Shepherd, at the end of every quarter gave us a test on what we had learned, and we liked that.

Then we had Lee Wilcox. He was a good teacher and he had a little alder down in his boot. If you misbehaved, he gave you a whack with it. He asked me to read something one time and it read, "stingeth like an adder." I read, "stingeth like an alder." I probably was five or six years old at the time.

Zachias. Oh, he was up in a tree! I had read my Sunday School lesson over with my father and he said he went up the tree because newspaper reporters were after him. Because of the press!

I told Lee that and he said, "Your father has a lot to answer for."

See, my father went fishing with Lee. They were great friends. Lee was a fun teacher. He was really fun.

Miriam was four years younger than I. Oh, she was a good sister. That's for sure. I remember when Della Ingersoll, Della Green, who's a nurse, was telling that we had a baby sister.

I already had an older brother and a younger brother.

But Della said that Miriam was the handsomest baby, the prettiest baby, she'd ever seen. I looked at Delbert, over in his playpen. One that Dad had built him, out of the old organ box that the nice organ had come in. And there he was. Pretty blue eyes. Nice little fella. And they said, "Oh, you won't like having a sister."

And I just thought, "Well, I'm going to like having a sister."

I remember the day. The mailboat went to Wood Island at the time. So the mailboat landed and my mother was in it. My mother had had her appendix out, maybe six weeks or so before my sister was born. This was a complete surprise to us, you know. She was still off to Seal Cove and she came back with the baby!

Gladys Green, Judson's mother, carried Miriam home. I can see it now, carrying her over. And Judson stood there and threw rocks at her. Judson's just my age.

She said, "Judson, you brat! You stop that! You'll hit her!"

I told Miriam about it afterwards and I said, "She was protecting you."

She said, "No, she wasn't. She was holding me up so he wouldn't hit her!"

They brought her in. Laid her on the couch in the kitchen. Big old couch that Uncle Prebble had made for Dad. It was about seven feet long.

She had blonde hair and it stuck all over her head.

She was a smart little tyke. There wasn't anything she couldn't do. If she had a hole in her dress, when she was three or four years old, she'd patch it. She made clothes for her dolls and she liked to cook and sew and sing. Be busy.

Now, we had a big field. We were told to stay there, most of the time. If we went to play with anyone, we'd go for so many minutes. But Miriam used to go out in the field and tie her sunbonnet on a block stalk. Then go over and play with the neighbour's kids.

So one day Mum was going down to the store and she told me to keep an eye on Miriam. When Mum got over, oh maybe about a quarter of a mile away, there was Miriam sitting in the path that went to the house, playing dolls with the other kids.

Miriam had a pet ox, Buck. He was a good ox, tall and strong. She used to lead him about by just leaning against him and she used to sit between his horns and ride around.

This happened in the fall, after the vegetables were in and the hay was cut and the cows were no longer required to stay in the pasture. Probably in October or something like that.

Miriam used to go down to Burton Green's to listen to the radio. We had a set but it had earphones and Dad put one on his ear and the other on the dog's. The dog would sit up on the chair and they'd listen to the news, Tom Mix, or whatever.

Delbert had already gone down to Burton's to listen to the radio. So Miriam started down. Well, her ox was standing in the path and, as you know, cattle stand tail to the wind. He heard her coming but he didn't think she was going to run into him. That's for sure. So she ran into him! She said he switched his tail just as she. . .

That's how she stuck her nose under his tail! And, by the way, she had the prettiest nose of anyone in the family. We told her it was a classical shape.

Anyway, the ox turned around and slobbered over her. She went to the house, pulling slime off her face. She was about ox-high then. About ten years old or twelve. She was always doing such things.

We heard so many ghost stories that you wouldn't believe. I used to be frightened to go by the head of that old couch in the kitchen because I thought something was going to get out and get me. But we never, ever let on.

Mum wanted something at the store and Miriam went down. When she came back, she was a wreck! She didn't have whatever Mum sent for and she wasn't very sweet smelling. We said, "What have you been into now, Miriam? What have you been into now?"

And she said, "Well, I was coming by the shed and something grabbed me and it bit me. It tore my jacket. But it smelled dead and I couldn't get over it. I'd take hold of it and I'd pull out great big strings of slimy something or other. I poked it and it gurgled! I rolled one way and it bit me! I finally got away from it."

We knew something had happened so Dad said, "I'll go over."

We took the flashlight. He shone the light and there was two pairs of eyes glaring at him.

Miriam said, "See, it's alive!"

Though what had happened, someone had butchered a young creature, a heifer or whatever. This was the custom on Wood Island then. You know, they butchered something to have for the winter. The winters were more severe then and if you hung something up in your barn, or in your woodshed, it would stay frozen all winter.

Anyway, what had happened, this man had butchered an animal in his smoke shed. Two dogs, Pal, who was Lydia's dog and

Annie Griffin's dog, his name was Bill, had pulled it down in the road. The dogs were fighting over it. Miriam got too close to one of them and he grabbed her. That would be a scary experience. And then she got all tangled up in the innards.

Now people probably wouldn't understand that if they didn't know what a cow's paunch looked like! She said, "I couldn't climb over it and I couldn't get free."

We were going to go to Green Island. The Shepherd girls had picked up a punt somewhere. They had advertised it and no one claimed it, so we had it pretty much for our own use and we didn't have to go taking other people's dories.

Although my father told me, "Before you go stealing anyone's dory, learn to tie a bowline and learn how to tie it properly." That's what he told us.

So we were going to Green Island and we did not want my friend's two sisters or my sister to go. We thought that they didn't know a thing about it.

When we went over to the breakwater in the morning, around six o'clock, a summer morning, there were the three girls! They were going with us. They were determined and my friend said, "No! You can't go!"

I called her aside and I said, "Oh, let's pretend they're going to go. Let's pretend we don't care. We'll tell them some things they have to do. Maybe have to help row, or whatever. Not talk to us, or something. But when we go over the sandbar, we'll dump them overboard."

Well, this sounds pretty bad but it wasn't. You can see the sandbar from here.

I can see Miriam now. She was sitting on the stern and she had a little strawberry box on a string, towing it along, and she was looking at that.

I grabbed her by the heels and put her overboard! She went under and her hat came off. She got that. One of her friends jumped overboard immediately.

The water was probably up around their middle and it wasn't a really bad day. There's a little current goes out across the bar but they could walk ashore. Although there's a little bit deeper place when you get next to the shore.

But the other girl was determined she was gonna go with us! We couldn't get her overboard. We almost upset the punt and when we did get her overboard, she hung onto the gunnels of the boat. We had to thump her with the oars and one thing and another. She went drifting down along the shore. She was a strong swimmer anyway.

We went down and had a lovely time.

When we went home no one said anything. I would have been surprised if Miriam had said anything, really. So my conscience kind of bothered me and I was so good to her. I think of all the good things I did for her.

Then one day, I was rowing. I rowed up to the bell buoy and I climbed out on it. The bell buoy is quite high out of the water.

They said they'd like to go up to the bell buoy someday but that they couldn't get up there. I said I would hold the punt in. So we rowed up and I jumped out and climbed up, took the rope in my hand. They pushed off and left me. The rope wasn't tied to the boat!

I stayed there all day. From ten o'clock in the morning 'til nine o'clock at night. The lifesaving station boat went by. They were talking and they were looking at the other shore. I rang the bell and everything. No one paid any attention.

But when Dad came home from fishing, he asked where I was. No one knew. Mum said, "Miriam, do you know where Annie is?"

She said, "Yes. The last I saw her, she was on the bell buoy."

"Well, what was she doing there?"

"Well, she was looking right straight up. I don't know if she just came down or expected to be taken up."

So Dad and Bernard, my brother, rowed off and got me. I think I had sunstroke. I tried to get a piece of kelp to put over my head but I almost went in the water then.

At one time, I thought, "I'll swim to the sandbar. But with the current going up by, I'll probably land at Ox Head Ledges or somewhere else. So I'll stay here."

You know, like the story of the old sailor my grandfather knew, who had so many things he didn't know what to do? And so, in the end, he did nothing at all. So that's what I did.

> He layed on a shingle, wrapped up in a shawl
> And I think it was dreadful the way he behaved.
> He did nothing but basking until he was saved.

So that's what I did. I remember Joe Green was there. Dad and he said, "Oh, you look like a sick hen."

This happened when there was no one living on Wood Island. My sister, Leona, came home. My mother had died. My sister and her husband were going to Turkey. They came home with their two children for a little while before they went.

We went to Wood Island. John was little, just an infant in the stroller, and Jody was nearly four. She saw all the houses and she wanted to go in. We told her that no one lived there. We went down to a cottage by the shore where Don Wilcox was and they gave the kids cookies and milk.

So we went to the next house and Jody said, "I want to go in there."

Leona, their mother, said, "No one lives there."

And Jody said, "I can see someone walking through the grass."

The path was overgrown then. We looked. We didn't see anyone.

Then Jody said, "See! He's going in his house and he didn't unlock his door!"

Leona said, "How do you know he's in the house?"

She said, "I saw him going in his house. I see him as he's walking by the window and he's going like this."

Jody rubbed her nose.

Now this man had died about six weeks before that and I had promised him I would see that he was buried on Wood Island. He wanted to be buried beside his Uncle Orville. Well, I was unable to keep that promise. He died in St. Stephen and he was buried there. He had a brother and a sister who were in their eighties or so and they couldn't come to the funeral. So she apparently saw something. We didn't see him.

We always went up around the shore when Sunday School was out before we came home.

So this Sunday, a friend of mine had been to Blacks Harbour. You know, babysitting during the summertime. She probably was about thirteen or fourteen. She came home and we walked up around shore. Well, she took out her cigarettes and started to smoke. And the boy that sang the hymn, he smoked. They were all smoking. They said, "Have a cigarette?"

I said, "No, thank you. No, thank you."

It wasn't that I didn't want to have a cigarette but I didn't know how to smoke. And I thought, "Well, I'll practice this first!" I was sixteen, Miriam would be twelve.

So I went home and my father smoked a bit at the time. Sometimes he smoked and sometimes he didn't. But I couldn't get a cigarette rolled. Finally I took a big fat fountain pen and put the cigarette paper around it. Slid the paper off over it and filled it with tobacco. It took almost half a package.

Then I went upstairs and lit the lamp because I thought it might take a while to get my cigarette going. I got it smoking in good style.

In came Miriam and she yelled hard as she could, "Hey everybody! Annie's smoking! Annie's smoking!"

I started after her. Don't know what I was going to do with her. If I was gonna push her down the stairs, I didn't have to. Our old house, it had a chimney but it leaked around it a little bit and we had a baking pan sitting by it, to catch the drops. Miriam ran out and she stepped in the pan! Slid down the hallway. There was a door at the end of the stairs and she went in that and burst that open! Her hollering!

I went down and Dad said, "Well, I would think that you would wait 'til you buy your own cigarettes before you start smoking."

That's all he said.

Then I said, "Yes, perhaps I will."

So anyway, I smoked all week.

And the next Sunday, when we finished Sunday School, they said, "Will you have a cigarette?"

I said, "Yes."

I liked it so well, it's a wonder I hadn't kept on.

I just wanted to know how to do it. My friend didn't smoke very long either. It was just a thing we were trying, I think.

I have this poem that's in this little book. This is something that, probably, I would have written from Sunday School.

> Teach us to delight in simple things, Lord.
> Thereby we gain knowledge in things profound.
> When You are teaching us how to be abased, Lord
> You are teaching us how to abound.

Keep our feet from forbidden paths
So that our eyes from tears may be free.
To worship Thee from not far off
But near, dear God, to Thee.

In this, our present habitation,
May we tread where saints have trod.
By Thy hand be fed as we are led to the foundation
Whose builder and ruler is God.

Help us in all our social joys
To do Thy will as girls and boys.
So that when the long afternoon shadows deepen towards
      the eventide of this earth's strife,
We may find the truth in the way
      that leads to home and eternal life.

As home we come with joyful hearts
Through the grace that our Saviour's love imparts.
The grace that enables us to be free
And praise and petition Father Abba, to Thee.

Still on Grand Manan in Seal Cove, I dropped in on Ivan Green. Unfortunately, Ivan passed away in March of 1997. I'd like to thank his sister, Beulah Green, in Brown's Flat, New Brunswick and his brother Paul in Truro, Nova Scotia, for giving me permission to include this material in the book.

Ivan Green

I was born on Wood Island. Grew up there until the war. Then I was away for five years.

We travelled the island. We rowed dories from Inner Wood Island to Outer Wood Island, all over the place. We was always in a dory. We had two pair of oars and we rowed. We weren't fishing, we were just rowing. Going from one place to the other. We'd go to the Upper Green Islands which is five miles or so. Used to chase ducks with the dories when we were old enough to go duck hunting.

The inconvenience of getting back and forth was quite a setback that way. But I'm on there now in the house facing Seal Cove. There's two big windows. I set there and write and watch the sunsets. And I watch the sunrises. I have two DL 95 cameras and I'll watch the sunset. When the clouds colour up real good, I run out and take pictures of 'em.

We played ball. The girls played as well, so we could have two complete teams. They could bat just as well as the rest of us could, I guess.

There was ten in our family, originally. Six of them grew up. If I'd 'a' made it, there'd 'a' been seven.

73

We used to fight with the Lower End boys. Got in a rock fight there one time, throwing rocks at each other. We drove them in behind the school house. We was out in an old garden patch so there was all kinds o' rocks there and they run out of rocks. So they had to send a fella down through to the shore to get rocks. When he started out we were laying for him. We put the rocks to 'im just as hard as we could. He'd have to run for his life to get down through there.

We always fought, for some reason or other. And then, the next thing you know, we'd all be getting along hunky-dory together and having a great time. Next thing you know, we'd be into another fight.

I remember one ghost story especially. Lower Enders believed in ghosts. The Upper Enders didn't. But I told ghost stories just the same.

I would go duck hunting in the moonlight, which is illegal, I guess. But nobody ever paid any attention to it. One night I was down to what we call White Man's Cove. It was getting close to high water and there was ten or twelve black ducks coming up that way.

I was looking out by the end of a log. You don't look over the top of one because, if you do, they'll see you. But I was watching ten or twelve ducks feeding up with the tide. They were a long shot but I figured if I waited another half, three-quarters of an hour, they'd be a real good, close shot. All at once, they were right in the air and took off! Quacking like some of them will when they get frightened.

I looked around to see what in the world scared the ducks and there was a fella standing on the sea wall. He was all dressed in white. I was exceedingly angry, him scaring my ducks. So I grabbed my gun and took over at him. Give him a calling down for scaring my ducks and warning him not to do it again. He was standing there looking out towards the Muir Ledges. He didn't pay any attention to me at all and when I got close to him he just faded away. He wasn't white, he was coloured. He faded away and the first thing I thought to do was run. What am I gonna run for? I'm standing there all alone with no one else around at all! It was kind of pointless for me to run.

When I got home there was some older men there. I was telling them about it and they looked at each other, kind of odd. Finally, one of them said that some time ago they had found a body on the beach. He was all dressed in white. They figured he was off of one of those ship wrecks on Muir Ledges. They buried him in one of those knolls up in back of that beach. They said from time to time someone would see him down there in the moonlight.

So I'm not afraid of ghosts or anything like that. I'm not afraid of seeing anything. I've roamed that island, down around there, day and night. All times of night. Never saw anything yet that I couldn't explain.

Before the Whale Cove road was cut out, it had grown up so that you had to push through the bushes to walk up the road towards home. I was walking up there one night and I noticed, about twenty feet behind me, the bushes were moving. Just the same as they would with somebody walking through there. So I stopped, pushed the safety on my gun, watching to see what was coming out through there. Nothing came but, by and by, a hand clamped on my shoulder, swung me around and headed me up the Whale Cove road. Pushed real hard on my back. Nothing pushed on my back again because they couldn't catch me after that! I went up through that road like a spirit! Never did find out what it was.

The men used to gather at Simeon Chase's house, down near the bank at Hardwood Cove, and tell ghost stories. All the weir fishermen rowed ashore and went down to Chase's to hear him tell stories in the evening.

Gerald MacLaughlin said he was there with a bunch of them from Seal Cove and he was listening to them tell stories. By and by, he looked around and they'd all gone. Rowed back to the weir boat for the night. He said he was too scared to leave, after them telling those stories, and he was too scared to stay there. He figured if he was going back to the weir with them, he had to get up there in a hurry. So he got up enough courage. He dashed out through the door and took up across that field just as fast as he could run, going up to the road to go down through where the dories were. And Chase had huge oxen there. There was one of those laying right down flat across the path. He fell over him. When he did, that thing rolled up on his side and let out a groan.

75

Gerald said, if it was possible, it scared him worse than he ever was.

He took off with all his might and plowed into the pasture bars. Thought he was killed. Anyway, he caught them in time to get back aboard the boat.

He thought it was a ghost when that thing rolled up and groaned like that, I guess. Scared him half to death.

When I was living just outside of Saint John, the New Brunswick government put on a creative writing course. Jackie Webster was the teacher. She lives in Fredericton. I used to write stories when I was a kid in school. Used to like to write them. So I thought that was an ideal chance. I would take the course. The charge was $7. When you finished the course, they gave you the $7 back again. I thought that was a pretty good set-up.

Now, I'm writing a story. "Out of the Sou'west" is the name of it. I take a young man from the rolling foothills of the White Mountains of New Hampshire, to make it interesting to the American readers. So they'll feel like he's one of theirs. He was working on a farm there and I brought him off of the farm to Wood Island and made a fisherman out of him. He was always interested in the sea when he was a young fella.

They started out from Portsmouth and Dover, New Hampshire, in a Bank fishing vessel. They was running up the coast of Maine. They were gonna stop in somewheres along the way and pick up their bait and ice to go out to the fishing banks. On the way up they ran into a real heavy storm and came pretty near hitting a ledge on the coast of Maine. So, to avoid that, they hauled her off about southeast and run for the lee of Nova Scotia. Hoped that they would make it. They were washing pretty bad.

This young fella got violently seasick. He laid down on the deck. Sea spray was flying over 'im. A couple of fellas carried him down below. He laid there, deathly sick, and it rained and stormed.

They got close to that ledge and they gave 'er both anchors and laid there. The next morning, it was bright and sunny and just a light ripple of wind from the nor'west. Beautiful chance there so they got their anchors up and sailed into Seal Cove Sound. And Seth, the Gunner they called him, he decided he'd been so seasick he was gonna go ashore and get his feet on dry land again. He tried to row the dory from setting up in the bow. It zig-zagged, you know, like it would down at the bow like that. He'd row with one oar and get it straight. By that time it'd swing back by and he'd have to row with the other oar. After a long struggle, the bow ploughed into the beach. He got out and took the painter and started up the beach. Gonna make it fast and stay on the land for a little while.

On his way up he caught his toe on a piece of rope that had washed on the beach and he pitched ahead on his face. A small point o' rock punched his forehead and made it bleed. So the blood started running down in one eye. But when he did that, this girl laughed. He said he got up, feeling like forty damn fools, and looked up the beach. There's a girl setting up there on a rock, under the bank. She was there waiting for her father to come in from fishing. She took a look at his forehead. It was bleeding a little and it was seeping down into his eye. She took him home with her to get her mother to patch him up. Stop it from bleeding.

(I asked Ivan to stop there so as not to give away too much of the story. He did admit romance was in the offing for the young man.)

We all know what a wealth of musical talent there is in Atlantic Canada. It's very common today to turn the radio on and hear songs written and performed by Newfoundlanders, Prince Edward Islanders, Nova Scotians and New Brunswickers. Our music's being played around much of the world. I think we have more than our share of storytellers and poets as well. My library of Atlantic Canadian books just keeps growing and a lot of it is good stuff, in my humble opinion. Lydia Parker lives in Castalia, on the way back towards the ferry. She starts by reading a bit from her children's book, *Memories of Childhood*.

Lydia Parker

Have you ever lived on an island? I have. When I was a little girl I lived on Wood Island with my Mum and Dad and a lot of brothers and sisters. We had lots of neighbours. We lived under the hill and the Griffins lived on top of the hill. Delia was my very best friend.

My dad was a fisherman. He had his own boat. Our boys fished with him when they finished school. It was what one did in those days. They fished for lobsters and made their own traps. We loved that time of year and loved to watch them work. Dad's boat was tied to a mooring pole way out in the water. He would row out to the boat and tie the dory to the pole. Off they would go, fishing.

On their return, they would tie up the boat, get into the dory and row ashore. Sometimes we were there waiting to see how many lobsters they caught. Once in a while Dad would bring some home for us to eat.

My two sisters and I had a trap marked for us. We were always anxious to see how many lobsters were in them. We were anxious because we got the money.

Dad let us play in his dory when it was tied up. We would push it off the beach into the water and paddle it back, over and over.

Would you like to hear about my school on Wood Island? It was a little like the school in *Little House On the Prairie*. Two people sat in one seat. We didn't have scribblers like you have today. Instead, we used a slate and slate pencil. When we finished one lesson we would wet a rag with water, from our water bottle, and wipe it clean. We had such fun. Teachers, at reccess, they let us mark on the board.

We played a game called Haley Over. Kids were on each side of the schoolhouse and we would throw the ball over and yell, "Haley Over!" If they caught the ball they would sneak around and try to hit us. Then it was our turn.

Dad and the boys made us windmills. They put them on a stick and what fun we had running, as they would spin round and round. The faster we ran the faster they went around. Sometimes we put them on fence posts or on the side of the house. What a noise they made when the wind blew. . . .

It seems to me, since I've grown up quite a bit, that I'm always saying, "When I was a little girl, I did this or I did that." Especially to my grandchildren. My own children too.

One day, I put a few little stories on tape and let them listen to them. My granddaughter was four years old and I said, "Well, wadaya think?"

And she said, "I luv it. I luv it! I luv it!!"

Her name's Holly and she lives in Saint John.

I thought well, I'll put them down on paper, off the tape. I tried to do that and the tape wouldn't work. So I had to sit down and do it all over again.

But I just wanted to get it down. I just wanted to get these words down on paper. And I wanted to get it published. I didn't care if anybody else read it. It was for my grandaughters, I didn't care about the rest. But I'm quite happy the way it's turned out. A lot of people are buying the book, so . . .

Dad had homing pigeons. He used to take them out in the boat with him. Write a note, put it on their leg and they'd bring it home. They originally came from Nova Scotia. I'm not sure which part.

Then, oatmeal used to come in a container about a foot and a half high. You know, so big around, like that. We'd stick a pigeon in there and take it to school with us and write a note. Tell Mum we got to school, you know.

One day, Dad took them out fishing and guess what happened? They went to Nova Scotia. They didn't come back home at all!

We had a pet lamb named Daisy. We had other lambs too but Daisy was white with a black face. This was about the time that I was crippled and on crutches and I got to stay home. I didn't go to school until I was eight years old. So I was around her a lot. She used to chase us into the raspberry bushes when we were going picking berries and she'd get caught and, "Ma-a-a," she'd go. We'd have to go and get her out. But she was always waiting around when we came home from school. Just like a pup. She knew when we were coming, I think.

I was in a cast around my waist, clear down to the knee on the right leg and just above the knee on the left leg. What happened was, when I was four years old, a couple of girls were pushing me in a hammock and I flipped out and fell outta the hammock and hit my hip on a tree stump. It bruised it, of course, but we didn't notice any limping until I was about four-and-a-half or five. So they brought me to Seal Cove to Doctor McAuley, our well-beloved doctor, and he sent me to Montreal.

It took a piece out of my hip socket or out of the ball, or something, and made me limp. Really bad too.

So I was there in the hospital, I think overall, two and a half, three years. But I would get out and come home for a month or two. Or I would go to Ottawa, to my aunt's. I spent Christmas in Ottawa once with my aunt and then she got word to take me back to the hospital. We got there and everybody was quarantined with chicken pox and measles. So I had to stay downstairs in a room by myself. Did I ever get attention.

I remember the schoolhouse from Seal Cove. The school children sent me a box. It had a string of pearls in it. And I can remember twisting and twisting that until it got so taut, it broke and flew all over the room. The nurses had to pick it up 'cause I couldn't get up and do it.

Crust 'n' Crumbs! We played that when we lived in Blacks Harbour. We had a big gym there and the teacher would line up two rows of children, facing each other. One side was called Crust. The other side was called Crumbs. The teacher'd stand at the head of one of the lines and she would say, "Crr-rr-r . . ." And we never knew what she was gonna say. So you had to be alert. You had to be on deck all the time. 'Cause she'd say, "Cr-r-r . . . ust!"

Crust would run and Crumbs would chase them and then so on and so forth. Sometimes she'd trick us and call the same name over and over. That was really fun.

My father used to sell his fish off Seal Cove, down on Mc-Laughlin's wharf. One day he got a fish for Glen McLaughlin and Daddy'd gone in and ordered up some onions. Glen said, "Lee! Did you clean my fish?"

And Dad said, "Well, did you peel my onions?"

I guess he hadn't.

Dad was really good at throwing rocks way up in the air. Way up in the air! So he told me. One day, when he was a boy, just as the bell rang, he got a rock and threw it in the air just as hard as he could. He ran for dear life and went in and sat in his seat. He just got in there and, *thump*, on the roof. It was the rock but they couldn't blame Dad 'cause he was sitting in his seat.

Poems. I have one about the bluejay coming to my feeder.

> The bluejay came to my feeder one day.
> I darest not move or he'd fly away.
> A beautiful bird, all shades of blue.
> I'm wondering if, maybe, you saw him too.
>
> He took some food and flew so high
> His colour melted into the sky.
> Once again I hear him shriek
> He wakes me up when I'm asleep.
>
> From early morn to dark of night
> He lets me know that he's alright.

And I have another one about sitting on the bank and looking out across and seeing the view. I look after a summer home, and I just happened to be there one day. I was sitting on the bank and I looked out across and I saw all this. So it's called

My View

As I sat on the bank overlooking the bay,
I saw the seals playing, the whales blowing spray,
The ducks diving for a tasty dish
And the boats out looking around for a fish.

As I sat there on the grass
I wished this scene would never pass.
And that all people were as blessed as I
To live on this, the most beautiful land,
The lovely island of Grand Manan.

Delia and I played together all those years growing up on Wood Island. And now her granddaughter, Winter, is my great-niece or great-great-niece. I forget which. When my little granddaughter from Saint John comes down, we always have Winter come up. So Delia's granddaughter and my granddaughter now play together, in a playhouse. So this is why I wrote this.

There is a playhouse, Delia, 'neath my lilac tree
Made by two little girls.
Winter looks like you and Holly looks like me.
There is no orange crate, they don't make them anymore.
Bluebells grow profusely around their make-believe front door.
There are no fancy dishes, Delia, only scallop shells.
I hope, when our granddaughters are older,
    their story they will tell.

I'm trying to encourage kids to write things down. And even when they start school, the very first little stories they write, I'm going to try and encourage them to keep those little stories. Put them into books somehow. My granddaughter's been writing stories now for ages. Since I have. And the little boy next door to her, Matthew, he's always writing stories. He's a beautiful artist. He's only in grade two and he's really good.

We're not quite ready to get back on the ferry yet. We're going to backtrack to a place called Grand Harbour. Wouldn't it be nice if land grants were still handed out by kings, queens and governments? Sure would make a nice down payment on putting up a house. It was the way at one time and it was no different on Grand Manan.

Glennita Hettrick

My ancestor was a Loyalist. He came from New York in the summer fleet that landed in Saint John about the twelfth of July, 1783. He stayed there for awhile. He taught school in Saint John. He also worked and lived in Digby. He was married in Digby.

He came to Grand Manan in 1803. Three families seem to have travelled together: the Greens, that was my ancestor, Cronks and Griffins. They seem to have been together in New York and Saint John and they all eventually came to Grand Manan. We have all three of those names on Grand Manan now. They're also everywhere else.

I don't know why they decided to come to Grand Manan. He had applied for a land grant in Digby, within the township of Digby, but he didn't get it. He came to Grand Manan and he had to fight to get one here. He had two hundred acres.

I have an older brother and an older sister. Eighteen months between them. Eighteen months between my sister and myself. But the way their birthdays came, there were two years between them in school. My mother wanted two years between us in school. I was nearly seven when I started school.

The snowdrifts too! I was very small and I walked nearly two miles to school. The snowdrifts were very large. With a walk like that and me so small, my mother also thought I was too small. That was the public excuse she used. The other one was the real excuse I learned later.

I loved school. Mona, my older sister, started school two years before I did. I learned my letters and I learned to read. I used to line the chairs up in the kitchen and teach them before I was six or seven years old. I was anxious to go and loved every day of it.

I don't remember the very first day but I remember one episode, in grade one, that got me stood in the corner for quite a little while. I loved my grade one teacher. I never wanted to do anything else other than become a teacher, because of her.

In grade one, when we had our reading lesson, it would probably be one or two lines. More than just reading, you had to learn to spell every word. One day I had to spell pussy willow and I didn't spell it quite right. I put an "I" where the "U" should be and I had to stand in the corner.

I went to a three-room school. Grades one, two and three were upstairs. Four, five and six were in the back room. Grades seven, eight, nine, ten and eleven, when there was an eleven, were in the big room. It was called that because the big kids were there. That school doesn't stand anymore. It's been flattened for a number of years now. The Central Wesleyan Church is built on that property.

I remember my father learning to drive! He didn't have a vehicle until after the war and then he bought a truck. He was going to learn to drive and you didn't generally tell him how to do things. He would learn on his own and he didn't listen to directions. He didn't need that. One of the most interesting things about his learning to drive was that he would forget he wasn't in the boat. He'd pull the wheel and wait for it to come around. She came around in the ditch! But that happened only a couple of times before he got the swing of it.

Grand Manan was settled on the sixth day of May, 1784. The island had a hundredth birthday and a 150th birthday and a two hundredth birthday. I thought that my contribution for the two hundredth would be to make a collection of poems, because a lot of Grand Mananers do write poetry. A lot of poetry has been written about Grand Manan by other people. So that's exactly what I asked for in a letter to the editor in the paper. I got plenty of responses. Some of it is very good, I think.

This was written by Walter B. McLaughlin. He lived from 1829 to 1906. He was a keeper at Gannet Rock Light from 1853 to 1879. Gannett Rock was named because there were so many gannets there. But by the time he was there, they were pretty well killed off. He wrote this poem and it's one of my favourites.

> On a wrinkled rock, in a distant sea, three white gannets
>   sat in the sun.
> They shook the brine from their feathers fine and lazily,
>   one by one
> They sullenly slept while the tempest crept.
>
> In a painted boat, in the distant sea, three fowlers sailed
>   merrily on.
> They each took aim, as they came near the game, and the
>   gannets fell, one by one
> And fluttered and died while the tempest sighed.
>
> There came a cloud on the distant sea and darkness
>   came over the sun
> And a storm wind smote on the painted boat and the fowlers
>   sunk, one by one.
> Down, down with their craft, while the tempest laughed.

I collected that from *Harper's Magazine* that we happened to have at the archives in the museum. It's a sad poem but the gannets are very, very rare here today.

I don't know the author of this one but it's short and it's interesting. It's called "The Cliffs of Grand Manan." It's written as though the cliffs are speaking.

> We have watched the stars for hundreds of years
> And we are as young today
> As when, unvexed by doubts or fears,
> Champlain sailed up the bay.

Champlain is dust and his sword is rust
And gone are men of his time,
Like the breath of a breeze in the whispering trees
Or a poet's idle rhyme.

We have seen the ships sail in and out
At midnight and at noon.
We have heard the drowning sailor's shout
And the fisherman's merry tune.

The fishermen, lo, they come and go
And others their places fill.
But despite the rage of storm or age
We are firm and youthful still.

This poem is by Iris Griffin. She was in grade nine when she wrote it.

Grand Manan, an island.
Quiet, peaceful, like a smooth river.
Beware of the current beneath the surface.
Once caught up in it, you will find it a struggle to break clear.

You may swim to a calmer area but the current,
The strength of the people, the place, will draw you back.
The village will captivate your imagination
And bring out parts of you that are surprising.

You might find yourself, once you can sit and think,
On a beach that has fog and mist curling around
    the face of the rocks.
Shifting each strand. Moving in the wind.

Try it. You'll like it. But be careful of the current.
It will change your life and hold you.

Just in time, we make it to the ferry and return to Blacks Harbour. The end of a visit to one of those places you just know you'll visit again. Now we head for the U.S. border but don't quite get there. We stop instead in St. Andrews, New Brunswick, and drop in on Helena Griffin. Believe it or not, she also grew up on that now familiar Wood Island. By the way, thanks again for the lovely lunch, Helena.

Helena Griffin

We were on an island and everyone knew everyone. We'd go to the school built out of wood and shingled but never painted. At the front of the school they had the boys' side and the girls' side. The playgrounds, the girls' side was the largest so that's where we'd gather after school and Saturdays to play ball. I pitched for our team.

Then I remember the flagpole was just to one side. We used to gather round that and they'd put the flag up. We'd sing:

> Never let the old flag fall
> For we love it the best of all.
> We don't have to fight to show our might
> But when we start we fight, fight, fight.

Inside, they had the hooks on either side of the door for the boys' clothes and the girls' clothes. They had a great big, old stove up by the teacher's desk. The stove pipe would follow the ceiling way down to the back, held up with wires. The ones up front would almost roast, and the students down back would be shivering and cold, until the teacher gave them a chance to change seats for awhile to get warm.

Down back, there was a long bench and they had the map of Canada, the map of the world and the map of New Brunswick. I can still remember the counties and capitals.

The teacher was up front, of course, at her desk. In back of her was the blackboard. We used to swear she had eyes in the back of her head. But our teachers, most of them, were class B teachers. They were teachers who had finished grade eight and wrote their high school entrance papers. Some of them would only be two or three years older than the pupils, but they were good. We respected them even though they were strict. You could hear a pin drop. We put them on a pedestal right along side of our ministers, who were supposed to be next to God, you know, in those days.

I think a teacher sometimes can influence your life. Like, my mother had a garden. Nearly everyone did but she had a beautiful garden. One day, when somebody brought a bouquet in, the teacher asked me if I would like to arrange the flowers. So, from then on, they were mine. Every flower. So I ended up being a florist.

We used to row off from Wood Island to Southern Head. The older girls and our mothers would take big pails and we'd all go in berrying. When we got our small pails filled, the older girls would bring us out and we'd play on the beach for awhile. Then, with our little jacket or a blanket, they'd let us lay there and it was our bed for awhile. We'd sleep. Then the older ones would come out and we'd get in the dory and row back home.

Seal Cove Sands

And the sand beach where you rested for awhile,
Made it your bed,
Was it on the beach at Deep Cove,
Just this side of Southern Head?
Or was it up more by the village,
What they call the Seal Cove Sands?
Did you stand there reminiscing,
Write love letters in the sand?

I had new boots and my grandaughter, Leslie, I used to say, "You are my favourite grandaughter."

She said, "But Nanny, I'm your only grandaughter."

So this day she called, I think my name was Hey Nanny, and I said hello.

"Hey Nanny! There's a volleyball game in St. Stephen. Can I borrow your boots?"

I said, "Sure. Of course."

So she took the boots. She wore them to school and the teacher said, "Leslie, I love your boots."

She said, "My grandmother's."

The teacher said, "I wish my grandmother dressed like that."

Three days later the phone rang. "Hey Nanny, there's a volleyball game on Grand Manan. Can I wear your boots?"

I said, "Honey, you have my boots."

"I know. Can I wear them?"

I said, "Sure."

So I was sitting at the typewriter and I thought, "Nanny's Boots."

There's magic in them there boots.
Now see if you can get them on.
Turn them loose and, on the back step,
They will dance until the dawn.

They will gather golden moonbeams and shiny silver sand.
They'll take you on a boat ride, across the bay, to Grand Manan.

They will tap and make you happy.
They will hop and make you cheer.
They will bring you joy and gladness that will banish all your fear.

There's magic in the wearing so be happy, little Toots.
Life for you will be all springtime
If you're wearing Nanny's boots.

It's only a few miles from St. Andrews to St. Stephen so let's zip over there. It's a beautiful day for a drive and for some stories from Burns Getchell.

Burns Getchell

To tell you the truth, actually, I built my first little radio back in 1923. My dad was a mechanic in the shoe factory and he always brought home the monthly edition of *Popular Mechanics*. In it there was an article on how to build a little one-tube radio. I think it was in June, 1923. Right at the time, I didn't have any money. Things were very bad back in those days, the late '20s and early '30s. Gradually I scraped up enough to get some parts. People that I knew, older men who had tinkered with radio, they had a few parts and passed them along to me. I had an uncle that had done a little tinkering with it and he gave me some parts. Eventually I got enough to put the radio together. But I needed a honeycomb coil. Seventy-five turns on the coil. I couldn't find any around but I had a catalogue from Allied Radio out in Chicago. I ordered this coil. Of course, it took quite a long while to come from the American side.

In the meantime a friend of mine, Reginald Price, had got some radio parts from a chap here by the name of Frank Ryder. Ryder had been in the Signal Corps in the First World War and became very interested in building early radios. These were all battery sets of course. Long before the days of electric. He had given Reg a whole box of old parts and Reg put it all together. But he was a little cleverer than I was. He didn't wait to get ahold of a honeycomb coil. He took a salt box and wound the coil on the round salt box that we used to have in those days. He wired it up and, I be darned,

90

he'd borrowed my diagram and he beat me! 'Course, Reg and I were friends for a great many years afterwards. He passed away a few years ago.

Anyway, he came rushing down. I had a little shack my dad had built for me to tinker in, eight by eight. He came down that morning, after he'd made the radio. Boy oh boy, I tell you, I was pretty provoked!

Eventually my coil arrived and I put the radio together. Then I could get the station. It was just a little one-tuber. Used what was called a UV-199 tube. I didn't have any earphones, so my dad went down to the local supply store that was here at that time and bought me a pair of Brandy's earphones. With this and stringing up a long wire in the backyard, I was able to bring in KDKA and WBZ, which was a sister station. Both were owned by the Westinghouse people and were at their factories in Pittsburgh, Pennsylvania and in Springfield, Massachusetts. Springfield, of course, was closer to us, so when WBZ was going it put in a better signal than KDKA out in Pittsburgh.

In those days, you couldn't hear anything in the daytime. Most of the broadcast stations waited 'til the evening hours to put on their programs. There were musical programs. Also some sketches and so forth. There was always a program for the ladies, cooking and so forth and so on. There were also news events. It was more exciting than the arrival of television.

Of course, I had the first television in St. Stephen. It set right in the corner over there. How I got into that was kind of interesting too.

My brother-in-law was delivering a tractor-trailer load of Christmas trees, along about the first of December, down to Boston. He didn't have any helper with him so he said, "Would you like a trip down to Boston?" I said I wanted to go down 'cause I wanted to see if I could find a second-hand television.

The family that we delivered trees to ran little fruit stores all over the city. They were of Sicilian descent, I think. Very nice people. I asked one of the young fellas that was helping unload if I could get a second-hand television. "Oh yes, my brother-in-law . . ."

Anyway, he took me over in his half-ton truck and, sure enough, I got a little Emerson twelve-inch. A little round-tube affair. The man demonstrated it and showed me how it worked. So I bought the Emerson.

We brought it back on the truck, all packed in a big carton. When I got to the border, since there was no television in Canada at that time, they had no rates on a television. They gave me a slip to show that I had legally entered it, but I didn't have to pay any money on it. So I got in scot-free for once. I paid $75 for it and, at that time, Canadian money and American money was about the same.

I brought it home and, of course, the only station at that time was again, WBZ-TV down in Boston. Well, you can imagine, hauling a television signal in over all the hills in Maine! Anyway, I put up a great big antenna. A wire antenna. It's diamond shaped and about 175 feet through the nose of the diamond. Sure enough, maybe two or three days a week, I could get WBZ in Boston. Then the rest, all you got was a snowstorm!

But everybody! Look, this room was plugged with people! 'Cause they'd never seen television!

As I say, Reg and I were always experimenting. Well, I had found a pamphlet that was put out back in those days. And this was spark! I mean, before there was tubes, why all the transmitters was spark. Used a spark coil to make the signal that was sent out over the air.

Anyway, I picked up this pamphlet and nothing would do but Reg and I would build wireless telegraphs. And what we used was Model T Ford coils. Now, the old Model T had a bank of four, one for each cylinder. These were vibrator type coils. A little vibrator on the top of them. They put out a pretty potent spark. So we took one of those and rigged it up with a homemade key and could transmit.

Then we used what's called an imperfect contact detector. This is two dissimilar materials, steel and carbon. The way we built them, we put two sharp-edged pieces of carbon on a little wooden block and laid a sewing needle, a steel sewing needle, across it. With that, we could pick up this spark. Reggie had one in his house — he was only maybe five hundred yards away — and I had one in mine. In order to communicate we had to learn Morse code. It was pretty sloppy code.

At this same time we built a backyard telegraph set. We scrounged wire out of old generators, from cars that were being junked. We finally got enough to string between our houses. It went across one street, using utility poles, and then ran in back of the houses and we had a telegraph line. So we could communicate either by telegraph or we could communicate with the spark coils. Actually, the telegraph worked better than the spark coils.

Of course at that time, around 1925, we had to be careful and not be on in the evening hours. That old spark was pretty broad and it would get into everybody's old battery sets, trying to listen to their musical programs and what not. We got bawled out a good many times.

Back in 1929 I got a handbook, an instruction manual, published by the ARRL. That's the American Radio Relay League, down in Hartford, Conneticut. It gave you diagrams of how to build a transmitter, how to build a receiver for short waves and all these different things. Well, I got that handbook and nothing would do but Reggie and I would have to build receivers. We'd already been building receivers for broadcast, so it was no job to build one for short wave. And then we, of course, built transmitters. So we got on the air talking to one another. Two radio inspectors in Saint John heard us and they eventually landed down here. Well, H.H. Brannen was a wonderful man. He was in charge in the Saint John office. He came down, along with another chap, and read the riot act to Reg and I. Told us they could seize our equipment. That wouldn't have got much! It was all home-built. And fine us $500. But Mister Brannen was a very humane man. He said, "There's no need of this. Send your $2.50 in to Ottawa, they'll issue you a licence, and the next time that we're in town we'll give you your exam."

And this is unheard of. But I was on the air, legally, without an operator's licence. The first time I failed the exam on code but I got it the second time.

If you look at the map of this southeast coast of New Brunswick, there doesn't look to be much distance between all the towns, villages and hamlets. That's if you can fly. By car, it's down, around and up all these peninsulas and around all these bays. At our next stop we're at Letete, right across from St. Andrews on the edge of picturesque Passamaquoddy Bay, settled very comfortably in the home of Herb Matthews. Guess I got Herb started in listening to CBC. I was in the car, ready to leave, when he remembered I was going to show him where CBC was on his radio. We went back in and there was the radio on top of the fridge. I didn't know where CBC was on his dial so just started fiddling until I found Vicky Gabereau's voice. That's it Herb, right between 90 and 92. He said to leave it there and he'd put a mark on the spot so he'd always know where to find CBC.

Herb Matthews

I've heard this expression over a period of years. This happened, possibly, close to a hundred years ago. I heard it from people my dad's age. There was an old lady up the road here and, of course, there was not that much money in those times. She sold a piece of property and had a few dollars. She used to keep it down her neck.

She took sick so they rigged up a bed for her downstairs, where it'd be handy. She had, I think, a son-in-law. His name was Newman. She knew he was after her dollars.

He told her one day, "I'll mix up your medication for you."

He went and mixed it up and he put some kind of rat poison, or something, in it. She was suspicious of it and said, "Just set it on the stand."

He set it there and he went out in the other part of the house. She just emptied it in the chamber mug that was under the bed. Set the cup back on the stand.

He came in and she was laying there, apparently dead. "Aha!" he said, "she's got it."

So he goes over and he reaches down her neck for the cash. She just grabs him right by the arms and says, "I'm a long ways from dead yet, Newman!"

And that was an old expression around here when I was a boy. Somebody that was, you know, sorta lagging or whatever, but would always pull his weight. "I'm a long ways from dead yet, Newman!"

We were carrying some fish to Eastport, Maine and I had an open boat. Dad, he was a rugged old fella, kept his hair clipped right off close. The boat was loaded quite deep. He was sitting just aft with his arms folded, to scare the gulls off the herring. We didn't even have a tarp over them. The gulls was hovering over and, first thing, one left a good deposit right on the top of his head! Well, I was waiting to hear the outburst. He just gets out a big old bandana, reaches over the side of the boat and gets some water on it. He was mopping his head off and he says, "What a blessing."

I said, "What'd you say, Dad?"

He says, "What a blessing cows don't fly."

It was good for a grin. We worked together for years and got along fine.

There was a fella on Campobello, Ace Brown. He was quite a character, old Ace. Everybody knew him. His wife got him a new pair of socks. The next morning he was getting ready to go fishing. Most fishermen, they wear boots that are a fair size so they'll be comfortable. So he takes the new socks and he rolls them all up and he pokes them way down in the toe of the boot.

She says, "Ace, what are you doing with those socks?"

He says, "I'm putting them in the toe of them boots. That's where they'll be time I get down to the shore."

Might as well have 'em in there first as last. Yes sir.

An old friend arrived here from California and he hadn't seen Dad for many years. Probably twenty years since he and Dad had

95

met. Well, he had a little briefcase and he had a bottle of expensive liquor in it, the little shot glasses and the whole thing. So he comes in and he talks to Dad awhile, then, "Would you like a drink?"

'Course, Dad would never turn down a drink, you know. He wasn't a heavy drinker but he'd take a sociable drink. Dad was telling me about it the next day. He said, "He had good whiskey but he had those little glasses that just held a snipe charge." So he wasn't too impressed.

Evidently, those old muskets is where these snipe charge things come from. They used to load 'em heavy for a deer or bobcats or whatever. But when it come to the snipes that they shot on the beach, little beach birds, they used a pretty light charge.

This is another old yarn. Here at the mouth of the river there used to be, way over a hundred years ago, privately owned wharves where they used to moor. You can see the remains of the wharves. They'd mill lumber upriver and bring it down in rafts and load those vessels. Go to Europe or wherever.

Old Bobby Lowe, a big old Scotsman, he was almost seven foot high. Bobby and his brother were giants of men. Well, he went to St. George with his ox cart. 'Course, he done his business and he bought himself a jug. On the way back there's a part of the road that the older people called, and I still call it that, Blackman's Woods. Bobby went to sleep on the cart. The ox stopped and laid down. Well, somebody come along, someone that knew him, and thought they'd play a joke on him. So they took the yoke off the ox and let him go.

Sunrise the next morning, old Mister Lowe, he come to his feet and looked all around. There was a seaman off one of the vessels walking to St. George.

"Good morning."

"Good morning," he said. "Am I Bobby Lowe or am I not?"

The fellow said, "I don't know. I'm a stranger here. Why do you ask?"

"Well," he said, "if I'm Bobby Lowe, I've lost an ox. If I'm not, I've found a cart."

So he must have had a pretty good glow on.

This fella, he went to go fishing. This really happened. It was blowing hard and it was too rough to go, a real bad morning. So he come back home and crawls right into bed, right cold, along side of his wife. She just rolls over and puts her arm over him and said, "He's gone fishing."

So that's food for thought.

Ghost stories! My mother, poor old soul, if she was living she could fill you in on ghost stories because the house that I was born in, down the road here and down towards the shore, it burned down when I was six weeks old. I guess that house really was haunted, according to different people. I heard this passed down for years. My mother'd tell us these stories.

One particular thing. Like most people in those times, and a lot of people yet, they put down preserves in the fall. They'd have these Mason jars and turn the tops on hard. They had a little way to get down to the cellar in this old house, with a trapdoor in the kitchen floor. Stone basement. They'd hear this click, click. This clicking noise. "Where's that coming from?"

"It's coming from the cellar. There's something down there."

So Dad'd take a lamp and go down. All the covers are off the jars! Here they are all on the floor!

Poor old Mother, she was horrified to see this. She said, "Oh, this place is haunted."

Dad said, "It was rats done it."

Well, he turned 'em on again. He was quite a rugged built fella and of course he wasn't old then. He turned those Mason jar tops right on, wicked tight. He said, "I'd like to see the good-looking rat'll turn them off!"

Put them back on the shelf and they wasn't no more than upstairs and they heard them coming off again.

Needless to say, they brought them up and kept them in the pantry after that. They didn't keep them in the cellar.

Another one. They were in bed, probably nine or ten o'clock in those times. This was late in the fall. They'd hear this noise, the way my mother described it, just as if someone had a lot of empty cans up above the house and dumping them down over the house. They'd roll down over the roof. That's the noise.

97

They'd come down to see and there wasn't anything. They thought it was boys coming and throwing a lot of stuff, but it wasn't anything like that. And there hadn't been anyone around the house 'cause, like all those old places, they didn't keep 'em as tidy as people do now. There'd be grass growing up close to it and the grass wasn't tramped down.

They'd hear pounding on the wall in another room. Or a rocking chair would start rocking for no reason.

But that house was built out of two by six timber, laid on its flat and mortar in between. The vessels coming out of the head of the bay, they'd have a big deck load of lumber. A nor'west squall of wind would come and probably part of their deck load would be lost. A lot of the old houses here were studded up with the stuff that came ashore. That one, she was built right up to the plate with that two by six, laid on its flat with mortar in between. But it burned. They always figured someone must have been murdered there, or something. It was a real old house.

We'll leave the Bay of Fundy shore now and head for the other side of Saint John. It's another peninsula, only an inland one — Kingston Peninsula. On the far side, next to a stretch of water called Long Reach, is a little community called, what else but, Long Reach. We're the guests of Beth Quigley.

Beth Quigley

We used to tell ghost stories around the fire and some of the kids would say, "Oh, you should write these down. You know?"

So, a few, we have written. We've been telling them for years. A long time. Probably in my teens I started them.

Around here they're very friendly ghosts I'd say, on the Kingston Peninsula. Not too many violent stories.

I'll start with a house in Kingston that belongs to Heritage. It's called the Carter House. The local heritage group took it over back, oh, in the late '60s, early '70s. They renovated it in the late '70s and then realized they couldn't leave it empty so they decided that they would rent it out to people. Just to keep it safe.

So the first family moved in, by the name of Pottle. They had a three-year-old and a baby. They were new to the area.

The house had these empty bedrooms upstairs. They'd take the baby's bottle up there at night, to save Mrs. Pottle coming downstairs. They'd just put it in this cold, empty bedroom on the dresser. So, the first night, Mrs. Pottle went in to get the bottle when the baby woke up. She brought it out and the milk was gone. It was one of those Playtex nursers, you know, with the bag inside, in the plastic bottle. She thought, "Well, that's strange." She decided maybe she had gotten the wrong bottle. Picked up an empty one by mistake.

The next night she tried the same thing. She had the bottle warmer beside her bed. The baby awoke and she went into the bedroom to get this bottle and it was empty again! She knew she hadn't picked up the wrong bottle this time.

In the morning, she figured she'd have a mess to clean up. After she got the baby settled back down, she and the little girl went in. There was no mess. No milk at all.

She thought, well, maybe her little girl was taking a liking to the milk, but she was quite sure the little girl hadn't been in there.

The next night they tried it again. This time they decided they would stay up and read, she and her husband. Just be quiet and see what happened.

When the baby awoke in the middle of the night, she went in. No milk in the bottle!

They just decided they'd give up on this plan and didn't think too much about it. As time went on, as they got to know people, they got to telling them this little story.

One of the people they told it to, his mother knew a lot of local history and the stories around. She and her family had been here for years. So she came back with the response that Dr. Carter, who had built the house, had a great liking for cream. He loved cream. Plus, he also liked to be one up on the deal. If he could get away without paying the farmer for a little bit of milk, he would.

I guess they decided perhaps that's where the milk went.

As they lived in the house, she would suddenly, at the foot of the stairs in the hallway, come across a cool breeze as she'd walk by. Sometimes her little girl would talk to an imaginary friend she'd call the man.

Now my husband had told me they were never told ghost stories when they were young. Not like our family. So I made some comment to his mother and she says, "Aw, I'll tell you a ghost story." So she did, after he told me they never had ghost stories.

It's just a short little story. It was during the depression years and she and her family, they were quite a large family, lived outside of Sussex. Like a lot of people they thought if they moved to the city perhaps things would be a little better. So they moved into Saint

John for the winter. She and her mother and father and her brothers and sisters.

They lived in a house in the north-end, I believe, on Main Street. It was one of those normal styles. You know, you had your kitchen and you went through a door to the hall to go up the stairs. She said they could never keep the hall door closed. No matter what they did, tie it, lock it, no matter what, when they got up in the morning the hall door would be open.

But there was no other sign of anything until the day they left. They decided, by spring, things really weren't any better in the city and they would go back to outside of Sussex.

They were packing up to leave and the father ran back in for the final check. When he went in, there was a little boy appeared to him and said, "Look behind the flue."

But the father never did! They left.

I can't believe it! And the house is gone now! It was in one of those areas that they came in, tore down a lot of the old houses. So the house isn't there.

There's a house in Clifton that we all tell a lot of ghost stories about. Doris Calder, an historian here, was to visit this house this past year and she hadn't been in it for quite a while. She had a daughter here, who used to live in the area, and they happened to drop into that driveway and the owners of the house invited them in to have a tour. They got in the dining room and she said that was her first encounter after all those years of telling stories.

It was that cold feeling and it followed them out through the house. From upstairs. So I'm waiting for my encounter.

That house was in the Wetmore hands years ago. Justice Wetmore acquired it in the early 1800s. He ran a shipyard and the boarders lived in that house with them. But the house was divided.

You couldn't get through one part of the upstairs to the other, without going down. Just for safety reasons for their family. The boarders could even come in off the back hill and come right into the second floor, if they wished. So heaven knows who was ever in that house besides the family. A lot of people coming and going.

Lately it was owned by the Treens. Years ago they had a post office in it and a store. Then the house changed hands. When we picked it up, as a story, a couple went in to renovate it. An older couple. They liked to do that kind of thing.

They were renovating and they had a hired hand who was a local person. He would never come back after dark. Never come back after supper to work on the house.

All they had in it was a table with their work stuff on it. Nothing else. Everything was in this one room on a table and this particular day the hired hand came back with a file for his saw and set it on the table. When he went back to find it, it wasn't there. It was gone. Well, they all searched. The three of them. The couple stayed pretty well there when he was working. They worked along with him. They searched and searched and couldn't find it. Well, 5:30 came, time to go home. There it was! Sitting on the table!

They eventually moved in and it wasn't long. She got up one morning and wanted to know why he was roaming around in the night? He said, "Well, I wasn't roaming around in the night! I wondered why you were roaming around in the night!"

This would go on and they thought, "Once we lay our carpets down, we'll be fine."

They put the carpets down and they'd still hear it. It was like someone shuffling along in a pair of slippers.

They eventually moved back to Ontario. A younger couple with children took over the place. It just so happened that my niece, Janet, went in there to babysit.

Well, all kinds of things would happen when she got in there. Little things that never bothered her. We were just amazed that it never bothered her.

One day she was babysitting. It was a fall, windy day, the rain had started. The baby was upstairs asleep and she was with the little boy in the family room. Suddenly, there was this terrible crash! Just like glass shattering. It woke the baby.

She ran downstairs thinking that she would find this mess and there was no broken glass anywhere. Couldn't find it at all.

Lots of little things happened. They'd be up in the family room, she and the little boy. The baby'd be in bed. And they'd think they'd hear his mother come in. They'd call down to her. Even, you know, so much as to hear the footsteps, the door open. No one would be there. She'd come home half an hour later.

One day in the fall, my niece was folding laundry. From where the washer and dryer were, you could see the kitchen table but you couldn't see the cupboards. All of a sudden, Janet heard the dishes rattling, like someone was going to set the table. And she could hear the footsteps, definitely a woman's footsteps.

Up until this time, there'd been a lot of men's footsteps people'd thought they'd heard but, she said, this was definitely a woman. She just called out, "Go way!" And then everything stopped.

One night she actually even saw something. She had put the children to bed. This couple, when they moved in, had renovated the third floor and had made it into a couple of bedrooms. It was an open stairway. A lot of these houses here, that third floor is a closed attic stairway but this one was an open stairway with a railing. She was just going on upstairs to bed and she saw this figure come out of the closet and walk down the hall. She picked the kitten up and went upstairs to bed.

It didn't even bother her! Well, probably it did but she wasn't gonna let on that it was bothering her.

They eventually got a cat and then they acquired a dog. I think, to hide some of these noises. But you'd be sitting in there and, some nights, the dog would just . . . his hair would just bristle and he'd run to the door and bark and bark and bark! At something in this upstairs hall. So it seemed to be the area.

The little boy told my niece one day, "You know, Janet, I saw a man in the dining room."

So I think children maybe see things that older people don't see.

My niece, when she went home to tell her family, her grandfather automatically said, "Oh, well, that's old Doctor Carmichael."

Now Doctor Carmichael was a brother to Bessie Treen who had owned the house. He was a pharmacist. I know he ended up his last few years at the Provincial Hospital but only died back, probably, when I was in my late teens. So not that many years ago.

A lot of the older people feel that's who it was. He was an eccentric character.

That house has had a lot of tales.

We were out on a bike trip a few years ago with some students from the school and we had come by this house. I was telling this story and one of the girls said, "I babysit in that house."

I thought, "Oh, no! I've ruined her!"

She said, "I have a story to tell you."

She said sometimes you'd be there and, all of a sudden, everything would come on. The TV, the radio, the tape player. Everything would come on together.

It has changed hands again, this house. I'm not sure who's living in it and I haven't heard. You don't like to go tell people. You know, when they move in, you don't like to go say, "Hey! Well hey! Have you heard anything lately?"

Now there's a house in Gorham's Bluff, where I grew up. It was the McCleery homestead and it was built by the Gorhams. This McCleery had married a Gorham girl so that's how they had acquired the land. It's the original house that they had built together back in the early 1800s.

It was a large family. The mother and father had lived there and the son, that was left to bring up the farm, was left alone. He'd never married. His name was Ivey. His parents died. The rest of the brothers had sort of dispersed, some to the States, some to Saint John.

He was alone this night and he had gone to bed. This house was also something like that other house. You couldn't get from one side to the other without going downstairs. But that was to separate the boys from the girls, apparently, in this house. So he was in the end of the house where the boys always slept, but it was where the attic door was. Up through the ceiling, like an attic hole. It was closed when he went to bed but, in the night, he had a dream that his mother was calling to him. A very vivid dream. When he awoke, the attic door was open!

He went downstairs and never spent another night in that bedroom. Built himself a little house out across the road and sold that house to his nephew. Said he would never sleep in it again. It must have been very vivid to him.

That's a story very close to my heart because it's pretty well where I grew up.

Years later, my brother was out hunting one fall. When Russell, the man who owns it now, goes back to the States they always put a great shutter system on it. So you could never look in the windows. You'd never get into the house. But my brother was hunting and he took a rest, sitting on the step. He said he heard the worst commotion and racket, like dishes breaking and flying. Well, he couldn't get in to see, so he was just waiting for Russell to appear in the spring, because he was gonna go right up behind him. Which he did. He saw Russell drive up, so he jumped in his car and went up behind him. He wanted to see what kind of mess Rusell was going to find when he opened that door.

Things were fine! Nothing out of place!

I'll give you a little change of pace. We won't go to a house. We'll just go to some of the road areas.

In Kingston, the road was changed years ago. It used to go to Kingston, up a further hill, out to Picket Lake, and then on around to Hampton. Of course, that was back in the days when people used horse and carriage, before hydro came to the Peninsula, when things were still quiet at night and people did listen. Every once in awhile, up by the Paddock House, it would be a hot summer night and they would hear this coach go by. And it was a large coach. They could hear the banging and clanging and the harnesses and the bells. It sounded like a coach with two teams of horses. Of course, at one time, that would have been the stagecoach route in through there. It would go by and no one would know where it would go. They'd never hear it come back.

But there was a story. Sometimes, after it would pass, they would hear the sound of shovels digging through the earth. Someone thought maybe that was a sign there was treasure buried up there somewhere.

Supposed to be a lot of treasure. You know, up and down the river, there was always stories that the treasure was buried. We used to search for it, when we were kids, on Gorham's Bluff. We were always told it was there. We never found it.

We used to walk up and down the river especially looking for, maybe, a map that was drawn on a rock. Things like that. If we'd see a little hole in the ground . . . we wouldn't dig too far.

There was a story, actually, that the man who owned the farm before us, he often claimed that he did find the treasure. That he dug it up and he looked at it and decided by the time they got into the mess with the government, if he ever told anyone he had it . . . well, he buried it again! We don't know whether to believe him or not.

But there was a story about the Gorham family, Harry Gorham, who claimed he found treasure. He even took a piece of it up to the tavern in Kingston. Of course, at one time, there were twenty-four taverns in this area. Boarding houses, inn type things. So he, silly like, went up with his piece of gold and broadcast it to the tavern that he had found this treasure. By the time he got home, his treasure was gone!

There's an area in the road here, in Holderville, called Ghost Hollow. There are various stories regarding this little area. It is quite a steep hollow and a few years ago the government came along and changed the road. Unfortunately, they blew the rock up which pertains to some of these ghost stories. There's different versions.

One was about a fella who always came at night to smoke his pipe on this particular rock. It was a habit of his. He had done it for years. Well, the man up and died and it wasn't long before people were telling little tales of spotting this man, sitting on the rock, smoking his pipe.

The community was very sure that this was his ghost, that he had come back. They found out later on that it was his brother and not this man at all.

I just very recently heard another story regarding a woman who used to go there to tend her husband's grave. That she would sit on the rock. She was spotted there long after she had met her demise as well, sitting there.

A minister came down through that area one night. Now, the ministers used to leave in the morning, would do their circuit and not get back until night time. He was coming back up through Ghost Hollow, heading home to the manse in Long Reach. It was a foggy night and all of a sudden his horse stopped. It just wouldn't budge. He couldn't get down. He couldn't get it to move at all. Then, while they were sitting there, this mist seemed to go ahead of the horse and pass and the horse went on its merry way.

So maybe there is something down at Ghost Hollow.

There's also a story around Clifton Rocks. Just like the minister, the peddlers used to go around here as well. A real twisty, rocky road. The government changed it as well but it's still quite ominous as you come by.

In this particular story the peddler, it was in the fall of the year, had made his circuit. That would have meant he'd have lots of cash and people knew that. He was accosted there. He was robbed and murdered and buried on a little outcrop of land, about half way around the Rocks. The men, we presume, who had attacked him, were never found. But it is said that, in the fall of the year, if you happen to come around the Rocks, you're apt to meet this peddler, with his moans, and he will follow you up until the first light at the Clifton Rocks. Then he'll go back.

I do have another house story. This house, actually, is a relatively new house built about 1928 by an older couple. Their names were Johnston. She didn't live as long as he did and they never really finished the upstairs. They had it plastered but not painted. Then he died and they were both buried in the graveyard, not too far from the house, in Bayswater. The house sat empty for quite a few years. Their children didn't really want the house.

Finally Alice, a girl who used to live here, and her husband, they had four children, looked into acquiring the house. The family was quite ready to give it up. So Alice and her husband bought it.

They moved in and started renovations. It wasn't too long that they were in that Alice kept thinking she could hear a woman's footsteps coming down the stairs at night. Her husband kept telling her, "No, no. We've put in a heating system. The house hasn't had any heat in it for years. It's just things creaking and stuff like that."

So her husband would never go along with her that it was footsteps.

She didn't like to mention it to her children because she didn't want to startle them. The children slept upstairs and the parents had made their bedroom on the main floor.

It wasn't too long until the children asked her how come they could never see the person that was walking upstairs in the hall. They would hear footsteps when they were up there playing and they'd dash out their bedroom door but no one was ever there.

So Alice knew then that they were hearing exactly what she did. Three of her children. One of the boys always was like his father, said he never heard anything.

This went on for quite some time but the more renovations they did the less that they would hear of this. Just every once in awhile they'd be in their living room or the kitchen and she'd feel this breeze, like someone was walking by.

Eventually, they changed their upstairs a bit. The upstairs was sort of funny. It had a bedroom with no window in it. A tiny little bedroom. They took this tiny little bedroom and another bedroom and made a family room at the top of the stairs. They had a pool table and things like that up there.

They had a little dog. The dog only ever went up once! Then he ran right back down the stairs. If they'd go up there to sit at all, play pool or whatever, he would sit and wait faithfully at the foot of the stairs. He would not go up!

Their oldest daughter came home one time to visit, with a child about one or so. They'd put her upstairs to sleep in the crib. When they heard her wake up, they both went up to see her. They could hear her talking to someone. When they went in the room, she had her arms stretched out to someone and wouldn't even go to them.

They still every once in awhile will hear things. A few years ago, they had guests passing through and they put them upstairs to sleep. Their children are all grown up and gone now. When the guests came down in the morning, they asked Alice why she would be upstairs in the night?

Rather than explain, she just said she was up looking for something.

Years later she was mentioning it to one of the neighbours and the neighbour said, "Oh, we know the house is haunted."

"Well, how come you didn't tell us before we bought it?"

They said, "Well, we didn't want to sway you from buying the house."

No one seems to know who it would be and Alice definitely feels it's a woman's and not a man's footsteps.

We meet another friendly person in Florenceville, New Brunswick. Lucy Thompkins lives on Main Street and she's a joy to visit.

Lucy Thompkins

I'm from Nova Scotia, near Liverpool. Actually, it's called West Berlin, the place where I grew up. When my ancestors settled there it wasn't called West Berlin. It was called Blueberry. The next village from us was called Puddingpan. Don't ask me why. There's still a little island, off shore from what is now called East Berlin, that's called Puddingpan Island.

I prefer them. I do. But there was a schoolteacher in the school there. East and West Berlin all went to one school. And there was a teacher there from away probably, I guess. She thought that because those two villages were settled by mainly German ancestors, they should be called East and West Berlin. I think it was a mistake. My grandparents never, ever called them anything but Puddingpan and Blueberry. They were not gonna be pushed around that way. No way!

It was a quiet kind of a life and things were so different from today. I think, maybe, a lot of it was better. Really. Most families were what today would be called extended families. That's what they would call it today. I grew up with my grandparents and my parents. And my siblings of course. There's good points and bad points to that. But there's one good point, I think. You learn to have respect for your elders and you learn from them. You may be a little bit annoyed with them pushing you around a bit and saying, "Now Lucy! You dust properly!"

My grandmother was fastidious to the last degree. She'd pick up a mat and look under it to see if I swept the dirt under it and all that sort of thing. But I learned. And to this day, if I'm going out, I have to wash my dishes before I go out. I can hear Nana say, "Lucy, you wouldn't leave dirty dishes on your cupboard?" You know? And that wasn't bad, was it? That wasn't bad.

Also, everyone had a job. From the little children up. We all had something to do. When I came home from school, I had to help fill the woodbox. It was a big, big woodbox. The next brother to me, he filled the big end and I filled the little end. And my older brother had to carry the water. We didn't have any modern facilities. We carried our wood and we carried our water. We had no electric lights, we had oil lamps. As I grew older that was another one of my chores. I had to clean the lamp chimneys every day and trim the wicks. Make sure the lamps were filled. All those things. We all had our chores.

My dad was a fisherman. He used to go with the Gloucester fleet. So he was away mostly, in the summer. So my brothers used to have to help with the garden and milking the cows. Haying, we all did the haying, from the littlest ones up. Even my grandmother. We all were out in the hayfield together. Everyone worked.

I never heard a child, in my life, say they were bored! That drives me nuts today when these children sit there, "Oh, I'm bored." Oooh!

We had fun. I had two older brothers. I have a sister but she was nine years younger. When she came along she was more of a plaything to me than a playmate. But my two older brothers must have been awfully tired of me. Wherever they went, I wanted to be with them. They were climbing trees, I was with them. If they went fishing, I was with them. We played hide and seek. I always played ball because I had my own bat and ball. So when I went to school, the boys had to let me into the team 'cause I was the one with the bat and ball. We had lots of fun.

I did say that sometimes I got tired of Nana telling me what to do. Sure I did. And I hated to wash dishes. Of course, soon as a little girl was old enough to stand on a little bench to reach the table, she had to wash the dishes. That was expected. I don't mind now. Don't mind washing dishes at all. My family'll say, "Oh, you should have a dishwasher."

Who wants a dishwasher? I'm the dishwasher!

Let's see. What was bad about it? Well, there wasn't any money. There wasn't *any* money! I can remember, we went to Sunday school of course and I can remember sometimes we could hardly find a penny to put in the collection plate. Don't talk about fifty cents, sir. Fifty cents! That would keep a family for a week almost. There just wasn't any money. That would be one bad thing.

We were almost self-sufficient. We grew our own vegetables. We had our garden. We had apple trees. We had cows and hens. We always grew a pig. I was thinking, I gotta tell you a little story about the pig.

We had a man who lived next door who was a rather grumpy character, Mr. Teal. A good, decent man but not very tolerant of children. Of course, the pig killing day was a big day because you always had people around helping. It was really one of the festive days. This man would come early in the morning and he would knock the pig on the head with a great big mallet or something. Then they just slit his throat. 'Cause they didn't want any bullet holes or anything like that.

So he got my brother Carl to shoo the pig out through the little trap door. Carl was quite mischievous, really. I don't know whether he did it on purpose this day but the pig went out the door backwards. Mister Teal come down with a big wallop on his hind end and I can still hear that pig squealing! He was so mad he didn't even finish the job. He went home. Dad had to get him back another day!

A lot of things in those days was very cooperative. Everyone had their own woodlots. Dad would cut his wood in the winter and haul it home. And then there was a sawing machine that went through the whole village and they'd saw all the wood. That was another festive day 'cause Mama had to make a big meal and all this stuff.

There were no snowploughs of course but they had to keep the roads cleared, for the doctors and the mail mainly. There was one man, I think they called him the road overseer. Whenever there was a big snow storm, he would start at one end of the village and go right through and knock on everybody's door. Every able-bodied man had to get out with his snow shovel and shovel that road for miles! It would be from home to Port Medway Corner. Then they'd meet the crew from Port Medway. That's got to be at least five miles. All with shovels. It was an interesting time.

I'll tell you another story. There was a shipwreck. This was the days of the rum runners. There was a rum runner ran aground down at the shore, quite near where our school was. I remember, when I was going to school, there was a rough road and we used to walk down to the beach to see what was left of the wreck.

Of course everybody in West Berlin, and I suppose East Berlin and surrounding territory, had their share of that liquor. I don't think there was a sober person in the village for a few weeks! A lot of them, they'd get a lot of rum and they'd dig a little hole in the sand and push the bottles down. I bet there's bottles down there yet! It was quite near where they had that big drug bust a few years ago. It was good rum. I'm telling you, my dad doled it out for months!

Gerald was in the army and he was down in Nova Scotia. Stationed in Aldershot, near Kentville. His unit was on a recruiting trip around Nova Scotia and they came into Liverpool. And that's where I met him. Love at first sight I guess you could say.

Us girls were cruising around. Girls can cruise, the same as men, can't they? Come on! They did! Whether they were supposed to or not! I made a date with another guy but I saw Gerald and he looked better. That was it. We just seemed to, I don't know, how do you explain that?

The people I worked for in Liverpool, their son had scarlet fever. Well, I never got it but it's a strange thing that Gerald did get it. I think the germ must have been on me. You would think that would have cooled him off. Don't you think?

We just met that one night. He wrote to me and then I didn't hear from him again. Wrote to me and sent me his picture. I thought he was something special. I really did. But then I didn't hear from him again for weeks. I was so mad I threw that picture in the bottom drawer and I slammed the drawer shut and that was it! He was sick in the hospital all that time, in isolation. Couldn't even write to me!

I was working in Liverpool when I met him. I was glad to get away from Blueberry because it's a very quiet little place and there wasn't anything very much going on. We didn't have a car. We never travelled or anything. When I went to Liverpool it was like going to New York or something, almost. And I liked Liverpool. I still do. It's a nice town.

Then, after Gerald started writing to me again, he was stationed in Saint John. So I went to Saint John and worked there for awhile. And then we got married. Then, of course, he got out of the army. We came up here because this was his stomping grounds.

Saint John wasn't bad. Saint John was more like the South Shore, foggy and damp. You know, just about the same. But the first summer I came up here I didn't think I'd live through it. It was so darned hot. I never, ever saw anything as hot as that summer was! I used to say, not to him maybe but to myself, "Oh! If I could only smell some of that good South Shore fog!" It was just a totally different climate. And a totally different culture, I guess you could say. Especially down in East and West Berlin. We were all almost family. That was one reason I had to get the heck outta there. I'd have never got a man! Most of the people there were either relatives or I knew them so well they might as well be relatives. You know what I mean? So I had to look further afield.

But it was a bit of an adventure to come up here. I like it here as far as that's concerned. I still miss Nova Scotia. We usually go home every summer. In fact, we had a little travel trailer down there but we sold it. Sold the little plot of land that we had. We just go down and visit now because I still have lots of relatives.

When you come into Mill Village take the turn that says Port Medway. You go down to Port Medway Corner and then go right on down to West Berlin. We always go in that way. When we top the hill, what we used to call Halfway Hill, you can look down on the ocean. Oh! It's beautiful! It's just beautiful! I mean, you just don't ever forget it!

If it was not for the river, I couldn't live here. I have to have water. I miss the ocean. I'll always miss it but, as long as I have the river, I'm okay. It is a beautiful river, the Saint John River, and this is a beautiful country. It really is. The hills and the valleys. I don't think there's a prettier place in Canada than New Brunswick. I really don't. I've got lots of good friends here and I feel that I fit in here quite well. But still, it isn't home. (Sobs.) I told a person, not too many years ago, that I still feel like a displaced person.

Now we head up through Perth-Andover and along the Tobique River to Plaster Rock. By the time I'd arrived there in that summer long ago, it was the end of my working day and I was beat. However, once I arrived at Lillian Everett's and we got settled in the kitchen, I soon forgot my weariness.

Lillian Everett

I presume the seed for poetry must have been there, someway. I did write a bit when I was going to Teachers' College but it was sort of childlike. I think maybe when I started back teaching, after I raised a family, and in our course studies, it came up. I remember I used to start the pupils in with couplets, just two-line poems, and get them interested in it. Then we'd go from that to four and we did some limericks.

Unless I'm called upon to make one for a special occasion, I just make poems as something hits me. For instance, I'll be sitting here, maybe Saturday or Sunday and maybe the snow is flying and you can't get out and I'll write one.

I've written poems on spring and, I don't know, just certain things pop in your mind. That is the best way to make a poem, I think. At least it's easier if you are so inclined. It's easier than if you're asked to make one for a special occasion.

When I knew I was retiring, I knew I'd be expected to give some sort of a speech. You know, with the retirement party. I thought, I'll never be able to do it because my voice'll crack. I'll get sentimental. So I thought I would make it up in poetry. I did very well until I got to the last verse and then I had to stop and take a deep breath and start on again.

There's one about the old schools. I was writing a poem about a couple who were having their fiftieth anniversary. Both dead now. I started with when they were young, then growing up, the school they went to and all that. I broadened out on how the schools were at that time.

School Days

Remember when we went to school?
We had double desks, as a rule.
The stove pipe hung by a wire from the ceiling
And produced a very nice, warm feeling.

Lunch was carried in a shiny lard pail.
Doughnuts and molasses, without fail.
Slice of homemade bread and a piece of meat.
A small bottle of berries. What better could we eat?

No Pepsi, Coke or Seven-Up.
We had a water pail and a big tin cup.
Our washrooms were located out behind.
Just two-holed affairs, a real modern kind.

No sex education was taught in that school.
We were taught to live by the golden rule.
At keeping law and order, the teachers were adept.
One thing they taught was the word, respect.

Should we misbehave or get out of hand
Her old canvas strap was then in command.
The teacher usually would stay one year
But if she met the right guy, she'd settle down here.

All grades were taught in this school we attended.
But then, school buses. This era ended.

I wrote this one about the terrible twos.

I'm only two years old this year
And I'm not very sure of my balance, I fear.
I'm so short I just come up to your knees
And can't remember to always say please.

I tried to climb up on the cupboard today
But Mom came along and carried me away.
She kissed me and took me up on her knee
And held me close and so lovingly.

I've tried to drink from my little blue cup
And what I spilled the cat lapped up.
I can't seem to find my mouth with a spoon.
Surely I'll be able to manage that soon.

At times Mom thinks I'm just being naughty
When I fail to tell her I want to go pottie.
She lookes very grim but doesn't fume.
Just hurries me off to our neat bathroom.

Now Dad comes home and tosses me high.
I chuckle and squeal and drool on his tie.
He then asks Mom if I've been a good boy.
She frowns and shows him my broken toy.

He said that's okay, I can easy fix that.
Then he sets me down on the braided mat.
Soon it was mended and he wasn't even mad.
There's no one so clever and good as my Dad.

I have one about fiddleheads.

The robins are back from the south,
Wildflowers now can be seen.
For the snow has finally vanished
And the grass is becoming green.

Poking their heads through the dry leaves
With a coating of scales thin and brown
Is the furled tip of the fiddlehead.
Just peeping through is its crown.

But a word of warning to the picker.
To ensure a crop for next year
Leave some on each little clump
Or our fiddleheads might disappear.

These emerald green fronds, when boiled
And served with poultry or fish,
Are a source of fiber and potassium
And known as a gourmet dish.

Drain and top with vinegar and butter.
They're full of vitamins and nutritious.
Freeze some in bags for the winter.
You've a wholesome green, so delicious.

This one is "A Senior's Viewpoint."

She might be eighty or eighty-five
But she keeps her interests very much alive.
If you think she's aged and perhaps senile
Just converse with her for a little while.

She keeps abreast of the daily news
After indulging in an afternoon snooze.
You may think her opinions are a bit outdated
On government plans so overrated.

Or the blare and clatter of a hard rock band
Which she openly declares she just can't stand.
But she likes to tell you of the good in her life.
Of being a caring mother and wife.

How Bobby and Sally used to play
With a homemade wagon in their driveway.
Of how the snowman seemed to grow
As they rolled and stacked big balls of snow.

She sighs and notes the great contrast
Between life now and that in the past.
And are the changes good for humanity
Or are they just appealing to our vanity?

So don't count her out yet.
She has wisdom to give
To all who know her, if privileged to live.

How did I come to write that? Well, I became eighty.
I was taught never to do work on Sundays, you know. So you
sit there and finally something'll come into your mind.

I wrote one, "Alone." You can feel lonely but I never feel alone.

I'm not afraid to be alone, it gives me time to think
And gather my thoughts together, while my cup of tea I drink.
It is then I write some letters, crochet or probably knit.
Or sew upon that quilt I started or work on that new craft kit.

If I feel I'd like some company and nobody comes to the door
I lift the receiver and phone a friend or
      organize things in a drawer.
I like to plan the days ahead, not dart about and worry
But try to make each day advance and rarely have to worry.

My son Gordon, who's in Ontario, had a fortieth wedding anniversary. Oh, what to get? Gordon was here one summer and he picked up my scribbler and was reading some of the poems. He said, "Mother, I'd like to have some of those." He enjoyed them. So I thought, "Now that's what I'll give them for their anniversary gift." I got a lady to make one of those books, photograph albums. They put the frills on it and all that material. A lot of lace and the like. I had another lady type out my poems. So I had that made up and everybody wanted to read those poems. I remember his secretary came down to the house one day. She didn't get a chance to read it at the reception.

I'm quite fond of this one. I had a wonderful mother-in-law. She was so good to me. She lived to be one hundred, all but five weeks. I made this one up about her.

My Mother-In-Law

Who's the lady with the understanding heart?
Who always was eager to take my part?
Who encouraged me when my spirits were low
And was ready to shield me from every foe?
My mother-in-law.

Who raised the boy in his growing-up years,
Bandaged his cuts and dried his tears?
Who reared the boy to act like a man,
To be the best that any boy can?
My mother-in-law.

Who was to me like a second mother,
Helping through problems like no other?
Who rocked my babies when they were ill
And soothed their crying and kept them still?
My mother-in-law.

Who said, "Go out and leave the children to me.
Visit the neighbours and have a cup of tea?"
Who cared for me when I took sick
And took the children on a picnic?
My mother-in-law.

Who taught me how to knit a glove
And interested me in crafts that I love?
Who showed me ways to economize
And alter used clothes to the proper size?
My mother-in-law.

A mother-in-law rarely receives much praise
For her deep affection and caring ways.
But I consider in fortune I've grown
Through that admirable lady I have known.
My mother-in-law.

All these things are true. She did teach me to knit a glove. She did help me out with the children. She was gone when I wrote that.

I did write one on her ninety-ninth birthday. She was able to absorb it.

The folk with this wonderful sparkle
Aren't always reliable friends.
It's plain folks so concerned, like you,
On whom, in real need, one depends.

Misfortune comes to everyone.
We all know you've had your share.
But you loved caring for you family
Though the dollars and cents were rare.

Two sons you had marched off to war.
Your heart was proud but burned.
Your prayers went with them ever
And paid off when they both returned.

After many long weeks of suffering
Your first son, by death, left us all.
But God must have needed him then
Else why did he issue the call?

When looking back, yours is the choice,
To see and count life's ills
Or dwell again, in thankfulness,
Recalling precious thrills.

And I, with pleasure, most surely recall
What you have been to me.
You've given me tenderness and friendship
And loving kindness, Mother E.

She was a great grandmother, great mother and a great mother-in-law.

This one is "I Just Saw a Bumblebee."

The bumblebee said, "I must have some fun
So I'll flit around and sting someone.
That shaggy haired dog has too much hair.
He'd never feel it anywhere.

The cat is snoozing by the stove right now
But she'd only utter a fierce meow.
I'll light on the horse who's peacefully grazing.
He'll whinny and gallop around like crazy.

With his tail held high and his hooves, clip clop
It'll be many minutes before he'll stop.
This is hilarious, I'll try the house again."
But he ended up dead on the window pane.

Can't go on a story searching trip to New Brunswick without spending some time along the Miramichi! I love the area but can it get hot in the summertime! Do we meet some nice people and do they tell us stories? Let's start with retired forest ranger Haywood Sturgeon in Douglastown and find out.

Haywood Sturgeon

When I was in school for some reason I had it in my mind I wanted to be a forest ranger. Even when they wrote this little prophesy in the high school yearbook, they put in there that I would be seen around the woods putting up Smokey the Bear signs. So the prophecy came true. I came out of high school and worked at the local mill up in Black Hill and then I went right into ranger school. That was in 1957.

As a ranger with the Department of Natural Resources, the priority was, the priority is, forest fires. It's number one. When you have a forest fire, everything comes to a halt and you deal with that.

Then you have forest management, which is lumber operations and laying out the cuts and cruising, seeing that the operations are done properly. Making sure their fire equipment is up to par.

Then you get into fish and wildlife law enforcement and fish and wildlife management. So we work with the biologists closely and do a lot of law enforcement. It's probably fifty percent of a ranger's time, law enforcement. Mainly the fish and game laws but then the theft of wood from crown land, trespasses. Certain times of the year were quite demanding.

The good part of being a ranger or warden is the variety. You plan on doing a particular thing this morning when you go to work and you may never get it done today. Because, when you get in there, there's all kinds of problems come up and people seem to call the rangers for every little thing that happens. Like, it could be an animal in their yard, a squirrel in the house, or a weasel, or something like that.

Years ago, we had two fires in Barnaby. One which burned a lot of houses, the C.N. station and boxcars. That particular summer, I started in Quarreyville. I was on a fire there twenty-nine days and they took me from that to Barnaby. And then from Barnaby to Smoker Brook. I started out on fires in the middle of August and I got home the middle of October! A hurricane came and put everything out! That was a real bad year.

But the next year, the fire in Barnaby was massive. Every day it burned the length of itself. One particular day I had forty-five men with me, three tractors, and the aircraft was overhead. About two o'clock in the afternoon the pilot called me and said, "Get your men out! You're gonna be surrounded!"

So I got my men out. We went to take the tractors out and the track came off one. So the tractor drivers winched the leg back on and I sent two of them out. We were the last two. I climbed up on the winch, behind the driver, and we started out. The fire was going across the fire break ahead of us and behind us. Scorched my shirt. Really scary! In fact, I met the tractor driver last week, after all those years, and he mentioned it. That was really, really close.

I've been living here for twenty years now. And three times, since I came here, fire's burned right up to my back door. So it seems to follow me.

In '86, the Newcastle fire burned close to here. I came home at three o'clock in the morning and my wife and daughter were asleep in the porch. And the car all packed with whatever valuables they wanted to take. They really thought, and I did too, that Douglastown would be partly wiped out that time.

It's really scary. The thing about a forest fire in a lot of cases, if firefighters are trained and good men, you can pretty well control a forest fire. But if you're afraid of it and back away from it, then you're gonna lose it. Our people, they put themselves in some pretty hazardous situations and they control the fires. In the case of bad days, you're bound to lose it. But it's scary. I'm telling you. When you get a fire that can travel a mile every ten minutes you don't want to be near it.

I'll tell you a story about a skunk. I went out to take my dog to the kennel one night and she ran in the garage and barked a little bit. So I took her out to her kennel and came back. There was a bag of garbage in the can in the garage. I thought a cat or something may have been around it. I went over and picked the garbage out of the can and put it in the back of my truck.

Saturday afternoon I decided to put a new bag in the can. I walked over and here was mister skunk in the can! He had climbed up on the woodpile and fell in the garbage. So I got a pole and put a nail in the end of it. The can had a handle on it, so I hooked the handle and picked it up and backed out the back door of the garage. But, when I stepped out the door, the bottom fell out of the can. And here was the skunk hanging by his front feet out the bottom. Of course, I dropped the can and he let go. I fell back over a work-bench just behind the garage and he got me! I ran around the garage and the shotgun was standing in the corner. I grabbed it and back around but he was gone. I never got him but he got me!

I walked over to the kitchen door and my wife could smell me. "No way you're coming in here!" So I hadda strip off in the garage and soak my clothes in vinegar. Some of them I had to throw away. Takes a long time to get that odor off. People could smell that a long time.

I'll tell you a story about a moose. Not humorous. There was a car, a convertible, just above Blackville when I worked there. He had hit a moose. So we went up to where the accident happened and the Mounties came in. There was two moose. We found one in the ditch and one on the road. The driver said that all he saw was just a mass of legs. And there was very little damage to the car, a lit-tle bit to the grill and a little slash in the top. There was a girl asleep in the back seat. She never even woke up. We took the two moose off the highway and the next day we got called. There was another one. He had killed three moose! And that's all the damage he had. There was three of them.

We did a lot of work with the RCMP, in drownings especially and searches in the woods. We searched one time for an elderly lady. She was eighty-six. We never found her. Her son-in-law took his family to church and she decided she'd go down to the neigh-bours. She walked down the road about a quarter-of-a-mile and instead of turning left to go to the house, she turned right and went into the woods. We were there nine days with as high as 250 men. We never found her. We found tracks where she had gone almost five miles in the woods. It's one of those mysteries.

When you work in an area like this, where there's a lot of salmon and a lot of salmon enforcement work, you get in some really bad jams at night. Not as bad as it used to be, but we've been shot at. Stoned, especially. The odd time you'll get shot at. There'll be a hole in the boat or they'll shoot over your head. But you can get stoned really bad, if they get you close to a shore. Maybe you're seizing a net or something. Some of them even make these big slingshots, on the top of a hill, and put huge rocks in them.

I remember one time we were out on a big raid. There was a lot of people there and a lot of enforcement officers. Mounties and Fisheries officers. This was right on the bank of the river and we were support staff. We had some canoes in the river, seizing nets. And the houses were all covered with slate shingles. They'd break the shingles off and throw them in the dark. Just like an arrow! You'd hear them coming!

I remember there was a Fisheries officer there and we were trying our best to . . . to stay alive. And a woman jumped on his back and got her arms wrapped around his neck and her legs hooked around him. You know. He couldn't get her off. What could we do? It was real comical. She gave him a real going-over.

One night we got a call about some poaching. Two of us went out. We found a truck and a net, and we were walking down along the river, off the road. There was some of these big grassy mounds. We were walking along and I stepped on somebody. He was lying between these mounds. I stepped on him and the fella behind me, he had his flashlight on and he said, "He's got a knife!" The minute I stepped on him a big groan came out of him. So I didn't get off him. We took the knife from him and he quieted down.

We deal with the same people the RCMP are dealing with. It's a better system today with radio communications. If you're gonna check a vehicle, you can pretty well find out who the driver is or who the registered owner is and if he has a record. A little better protection today.

124

I went to work among my own people and I worked for seventeen years among my own. Right in my own village. My policy was treat everybody the same. It didn't matter if it was an aunt or an uncle, they got the same treatment. I was there to do what I had to do and I done it. And they respect me for that.

I remember I got a call one night from one of the rangers. He told me that he expected that he was gonna find three moose shot and he wanted some backup. So I got a crew together and went down. When I got there, this was in the winter, he was at the road, at the snowbank and he had seized three snowmobiles and three moose and arrested the three fellas. And the moose were all at the side of the road. I said, "How did you ever do that?"

Three men and three snowmobiles! To get them out of the woods! You know, if you put them on the snowmobiles, they'd take off on you.

And he said, "I took their mitts!"

I said, "You what?"

He said, "I took their mitts!"

So they couldn't go very far because they'd freeze their hands. They'd have to go a little ways and then stop to warm their hands.

Everybody makes mistakes. As much as I was involved with law enforcement and I did a lot of teaching our staff over the years. It was just after two Mounties had been killed in Fredericton. One of the Mounties I knew really well. Had worked with him. Knew him since he was a boy.

Just after that, I was called to Baie-Ste-Anne to search a house. At that time we had blanket search warrants. A moose had been brought out to one side of the road, across from a fella's house, and blood led right to the house. So we went down and searched. I went in the house and the lady was there. It was just a two-room thing with a partition down where the bedrooms were and blankets hanging over the bedroom doors. The kids were screaming and she was screaming. The husband wasn't home. She was screaming, "You're not gonna take my sheep meat!" She had sheep, mutton, in the freezer. So I said we'd wait. We sent for him and we waited 'til he come home.

He was really upset but he cooperated and he gave me his full statement. They had found the moose in the woods, he told me. Snared. He shot it and they carried it out, the two of them. Across

125

the road from the house, he chopped it up with an axe and carried it home. Put it in the freezer. That was the mutton! Anyhow, I asked him, "Do you have the rifle?"

"Yes."

"Will you give it to me?"

"Yes, it's in the house."

So we went in. And I made the mistake. I never did it before or after. He went in the bedroom alone. I should never have done it. And if you ever heard the action of a rifle opening! I'll never forget it. I heard him in the bedroom when the blanket closed over the door when he walked in it. I heard the action open on the rifle and what happened to those two Mounties went through my mind. Just in an instant. I thought I was dead. I wasn't armed at the time and he was going to come out of that room with a rifle! And he did come out. But he had it by the barrel, up by the sight. Brought it over and handed it to me. And I'm telling you, talk about a fella being taught a lesson! Never again!

We were doing some surveillance on an orchard. They were night hunting in the orchard and it was pouring rain. There was four of us. Two went in one way. There was a warden with me and we went in another way. Not very far from my home. So we spent all night in the orchard. About three o'clock in the morning we decided to leave. We were walking down through the orchard and it was pitch dark, pouring rain. All of a sudden, we walked right up to this thing. It jumped in front of us. A big snort! And it was a black horse. We almost walked on him. Talk about taking a fright out of you!

Then we got over to the fence and the old fella who lived there he was a big, tall, tall man. He made his fences real tall. Real high. We had a hard time to get over the fence. We walked out to where I had parked my truck and went home.

When I got up the next morning my wife wouldn't speak to me. It was about a week before I could find out what I had done. Finally, after a lot of coaxing, she told me.

There was a hooker that lived on the road that we were working on. Somebody had called. Saw my truck parked just down the road from her place and told my wife that I was at this hooker's house!

I'm telling you, she still doesn't believe me, I don't think.

My son was in an environmental science class at Miramichi Valley. The teacher decided he wanted to take his class on a river, to run a river by canoe. And he decided he'd go on Bartholomew River. Now this was in May and I had agreed to go bring one of the vehicles back, along with another teacher. So when we got up behind Doaktown, on one of the branches of the Bartholomew, it had rained all night, hard. That river was rising really fast. So I asked him not to go because those rivers run off fast. They come up fast and run off fast. You can get into a flooding situation really easy there. He assured me they were all experienced and they were going.

Well, before they were out of sight, one canoe upset. We helped them ashore and they dumped their canoe. They wanted to continue, so we left.

Sunday morning, they should have been home. This was around ten or eleven o'clock and there was no sign of them. I got one of the other rangers and an outboard. We travelled thirty miles up Bartholomew and we reached what they call the branches, as far as we could get with the outboard. No sign of them. We were really concerned then. We didn't find anything at all. No debris. So we knew something had happened.

We came back to Blackville and I informed the RCMP in Doaktown. Then I went up to Doaktown. The RCMP officer asked me what I needed, after I explained, and I told him I needed a helicopter. He tried for the RCMP chopper but the ceiling was too low, so he got a Search and Rescue helicopter out of Chatham.

In the meantime, just before the chopper got there, my son and another boy had left the group. They had waded through snow and swam Mud Brook to get out to the road. They finally got a drive out to the nearest phone and they called the RCMP office. I was there so he had told me where they were and that they were in pretty bad shape. One girl especially wasn't well at all.

The helicopter came and we took off. When we saw the fires, the pilot circled the area and I found a clearing that was close. So he put the helicopter down. I'd taken a compass bearing so I could get to them the shortest way from this clearing. I had to wade a brook, cross through a moose yard, a big thicket, and across a swamp. I finally got to them. There was seventeen kids left there, out of twenty -one, and they were a really bad mess. Everyone of them but my son and another boy, they had all upset. They were soaked. They had burned their sneakers and lifejackets and whatever they could to keep the fires going and try to keep warm. The girl was suffering from hypothermia and I knew we couldn't carry her out. So I called the helicopter. They circled, came right over the top of us, and dropped a cable down. One of the crew come down with the cable. We put a harness on her and they took her up and took her out to an ambulance. The kid that come down, he was dressed in a real nice flight suit. I asked him, "They're gonna come back for you?"

He said, "Oh no. I'm staying with you."

I said, "Look how you're dressed."

He said, "Don't worry about me."

He was a good kid. He was ready to help.

So we got the kids all together and gathered up what we could have them carry and we went out. They were just exhausted! And soaked! We waded through snow and across a brook right up to the knees. That icy water. We got out on an old road and it was all ice on one side where the snow had drifted in the winter and they slipped and they fell. God, what a sad looking crew. Got them out to the chopper and loaded them all in. Put seventeen of them in it. It was one of those big Search and Rescue jobs. He took them out and returned for us. Just lucky there was nobody drowned.

The little girl that we took out first, she told me that when the canoe upset and she realized she was on the bottom, she looked up and all she could see was limbs, branches. She was under a tree that was across the river. The first time she surfaced, my son and the other boy that was with him caught her. Got a rope on her and they towed her ashore.

The next week, when the water dropped, we went in after the canoes. There was five canoes. Their sleeping bags . . . now this is how high the water was . . . their sleeping bags were way down. You could see these blue or red sleeping bags down through the alders where they had washed in. They had floated in there. We left them. You couldn't lift them they were that heavy.

It was quite an experience. Something that you would see on TV. You'd never think you would live to experience something like that. It's something that's stuck in my mind all my life. Lucky! Lucky!

One of the canoes was a twenty-six-footer. A big canoe. And the river is really crooked. There's right-angle turns on it. That canoe, once the water had dropped, it wouldn't go round the turns.

One turn we came to, there was a big elm tree across. One of the rangers, he'd do most anything. We had a power saw and he undertook to cut the tree up. When it got almost through it, of course, the tree settled and jammed the saw. So he took the motor off and left the bar and the chain there. I said, "Well, we'll come back. We'll have to leave it there."

He said, "Oh no. You fellas just go down the river a little bit. I can get that."

He's not afraid of anything. He reached in his packsack and he got a stick of dynamite. He tied the dynamite under the bottom of the tree, where the saw was gonna come through, and he ran his wires back to the stump. Probably twenty feet, twenty-five feet away from where the dynamite would be. And he tied a rope on the bar of the saw. He had to be fast because he had a flashlight battery to touch the wires to, to put the dynamite off. He had to do that and then grab the rope and pull it. So he touched the battery. The dynamite went off and he grabbed the rope. Of course, the dynamite shoved the tree up out of the water a little bit. He was fast enough that when he pulled the rope he pulled the bar out!

A train had hit a moose just outside of Newcastle and it had been there for some time. It was really, really spoiled bad. A bad mess. You couldn't move it. It would fall apart. So the same ranger was there and he said, "I can move that moose."

Again, he digs in his packsack and this time he's got a little more powder. He loads that moose and he was good at it. He knew just where to set the charges. He put the dynamite all around the moose, set it just where he wanted it, run his wires back and touched the battery.

That moose went up in the air, across the tracks and down in the alders! The whole moose!

I like some of the local place-names around Miramichi. Douglas-town, where we just were, South Esk, Bartibog Bridge, Burnt Church and Red Bank, where we're headed now to meet Tom Donovan, another teacher.

Tom Donovan

There were a lot of storytellers and poets around the Miramichi. It was a lumbering community where men went to the woods and worked all winter in the lumbering camps, a rather dangerous situation, and brought the logs out in the spring river drives. Those experiences they had created the people. Characters, I suppose. Minor heroes of sorts. People who could break up the logs. Run the logs on the roughest waters, Hell's Gate and all of these here. Of course, many of them died as well.

It was also a very Celtic background. Irish and Scots. The Irish brought with them many of the superstitions of the Celts. I was more familiar with the Irish group of people and they were very superstitious, believing in all kinds of strange creatures of the next world. Of course their Christian religions as well gave them a certain amount of spiritual belief in the supernatural.

One of the characters, around the time of the First World War, was Bill Duncan. Actually, Bill Duncan came to the area. He was a kind of a hermit, an eccentric. There were various rumours where he came from, or he had killed someone somewhere, or that he was shell-shocked from the first war.

He built a log cabin way up in the woods and was a trapper. Lived off the trapping up in the Central Lakes area. He didn't like people. He was a loner and he didn't want people coming to visit him.

He travelled a lot. There were rumours that he was also a deserter.

In any case, he had a very cold, fishy stare. This is how the locals described him. That he had a scary look about him. A goat's eyes, one person said.

I remember him in the '40s, when I was a child. He would come down the old gravel road, with a gray beard and he had a bundle on his back. He always carried furs down or traps or something. Children were very afraid of him. I remember children, they'd be out on the gates. He would come by and he would look at them with that cold, fish-eyed stare and the children would run. I remember that. Maybe there was nothing to it but we believed it to be so. Of course, if we believed it to be so, it was our experience. Nobody led us to believe otherwise.

Duncan, he had a pet squirrel and it was his only friend. Some of the locals said that he really didn't have friends. He didn't want any. But he had this pet squirrel and the squirrel would sit on the old plank table and eat with Duncan. He would take bread out of Duncan's hands.

Another trapper, an acquaintance of his not a friend, Sandy Gratton, came to Duncan's one cold, winter night, from the trap lines. Snowshoeing. He imposed himself upon Duncan to stay the night because it was late and cold and he was tired.

He didn't know of this pet squirrel and, when Gratton was eating at the table, Duncan went out to get a bucket of water. While he was out, this squirrel jumped down off of the rafter, normal procedure with Bill Duncan, and he grabbed this slice of bread from Gratton. Gratton was quite upset with this and quite surprised at this wild squirrel. He impaled him on the plank table with his fork!

At that time, Duncan returned and saw his pet squirrel, his only friend, impaled! This squirming squirrel, impaled with a fork, on his old plank table! Of course, he became enraged and he grabbed a hunting knife and chased Sandy out into the winter night. Sandy fled, fearing for his life and he had to walk all the way to the village. A long way at that time. Sandy never returned to Bill Duncan's log cabin again.

That was a true story.

I think everyone who grew up without media became a story-teller of sorts. Certainly they listened to people who were storytell-ers at the little country stores. You'd sit there and people would tell you.

I believed, for example, the Dungarvon Whooper ghost to be a fact until I was probably in high school. I believed it to be the truth.

"The Dungarvon Whooper" is a poem by Michael Whalen, a local poet, fairly well-known throughout this part of the country. He was self-taught. Born in 1858 and lived his life in this area ex-cept for a short period in Minnesota with his brothers. He taught school. He was a bookkeeper.

He was an angular man, about six-foot-seven. Tall, rather wiry character. Very pleasant fellow, though. Rather a gentle scholar if you wish. He died, impoverished, in the poor house in 1937. Was buried in a pauper's grave.

Amongst his poems, one of the best known is "The Dungarvon Whooper." It was based on an actual story.

Around 1850 a young man from Prince Edward Island came to cook in a lumber camp up the Dungarvon River, a tributary of the Renous. They stayed most of the winter in these camps. While he was there alone with the foreman, he took suddenly ill and died. When the crew came back that night they found that their cook had died rather strangely and mysteriously. One thing they did notice was that his money belt was missing. At that time, people carried money belts.

They suspected, of course, that he in actual fact had been mur-dered. Because why would the money belt be missing?

The story is that he was to be hauled out to the graveyard, miles out, by sleigh in the winter. A great storm appeared and in the poem, "The Dungarvon Whooper," the author talks about the death and he says,

> A sad tragedy took place and death won another race
> When the young cook swiftly passed to the unknown.
> In the day of long ago comes the weird tale of woe,
> The sad and solemn subject of my song.

Whalen had a very good understanding of the forest, the deep forest. It was a haunting place. We think of the forest today as a place of recreation but the early pioneer feared the forest. The for-est was a place where savage creatures lived. Eastern panther was here, the bear and wolves. People could be killed and children oft-time were, especially if they got lost. They feared the forest. You could easily burn to death in a fire.

The great Miramichi fire, in 1825, burned hundreds of people to death. It burned 135 miles in eight hours. There was no escaping it. So the forest had a kind of an evil connotation in many respects, even though it was their livelihood.

Whalen, in his opening verses to "The Dungarvon Whooper," he described the forest.

> Far within the forest scene
> Where the trees forever green
> Form a contrast to the beech and birches gray.
> Where the snow lies white and deep
> And the songbirds seem to sleep
> And cease their sweetest singing all the day.
>
> Where the mighty monster moose,
> Of limbs long and large and loose,
> Through the forest sweeps with stride both swift and strong.
> Where the caribou and deer swim the brooks so crystal clear
> And where the dark and deep Dungarvon sweeps along.

It was in this scene, when the cook died, that they prepared to take him away to the graveyard to be buried in Renous. And a great storm came up. Whalen says it in his poem.

> Fast fell the driven snow
> While the wildest winds did blow,
> 'Til four feet deep lay upon the ground.
> So that on the burial day
> To the graveyard far away
> To bear the corpse, impossible, was found.

So the workers gave the young cook a woodsman's grave. It's still there today. It's near a spring called Whooper's Spring. The young cook was buried there and when the crew returned that evening, they heard strange sounds. Of course, they were afraid and superstitious. There were sounds in the forest. Screech owls and the eastern panther, which had a strange sound. It disappeared from this area sixty or seventy years ago. It was no doubt those sounds but in their minds, it was the spirit of the slain cook seeking vengeance for what had happened to him. That he would not rest.

One of the beliefs amongst the community was that people who are murdered, or grave injustice is done to them, that their souls would not rest until justice was done.

When he says,

> Such fearful whoops and yells the forest fill,
> Pale and ghastly was each face.
> We shall leave this fearful place
> For this camp unto the demon does belong.
> Ere the dawning of the day
> We shall hasten far away
> From where the dark and deep Dungarvon sweeps along.

As the story goes, they left that camp and did not return. That was around 1850. For many, many years, the settlers who lived away up in the wilderness — those tributaries were settled back then and they no longer are — any sound they heard in the forest at night, they believed it to be the ghost.

It caused enough unrest amongst the people that by 1890 the local parish priest at Renous, Father Edward Murdoch, got permission to travel up to the woodsman's grave and perform the rite of exorcism. The story goes that the ghost, his soul, was quiet. If they believed it to be so, of course, it was.

> 'Til beside the grave stand God's good man with lifted hand
> And pray that he, these sounds would not prolong.
> That those fearful sounds should cease
> And the region rest in peace
> Where the dark and deep Dungarvon sweeps along.

A train that travelled between Newcastle and Fredericton, around 1890 and the early part of the twentieth century, was named after the Whooper. It was called the Whooper because of its haunting sound that was supposed to have some similarities to the sounds these people thought they heard.

Now the province of New Brunswick has listed the grave site as some sort of protected property. There's a little sign up and so on. Even when I was a boy, in the '40s and early '50s, it was a kind of place that most people avoided, even though you didn't believe it. Just in case it was true!

Whalen was a well-liked person. Unlike Joe Smith or, in later years, Larry Gorman. A lot of people didn't like them because they did some unpleasant things. They wrote some unpleasant poems about them. Whalen was brighter, more scholarly. He was a very gentle, kind man. Life was harsh to him, for somebody of such talent. His young girlfriend died and he never went with anyone else again. He started drinking. But he never felt that life had been hard to him. His main role in life, as he said, was to depict the Miramichi and its people in the most beautiful manner he could. And he did.

As I say, on our river there were storytellers and poets. Joe Smith was what we would call a rogue poet. He was a wild individual but he had skills in composing poetry and ballads about people. Smith ran away from home when he was fourteen. Went away to the Canadian west and the U.S.A. and travelled a lot. He got the name of Roving Joe and he called himself that. He fished and hunted, trapped away up into the wilderness. Up into the Central Lakes which, at that time, was a long way. You had to walk in on foot.

Smith lived like an animal in the forest. He was tough. A big man. Very strong. They said he could carry a barrel of pork on his shoulders.

He was quite a scrapper. Nobody would mingle with Smith. He was very quick. He could turn what we call flying hand springs. A man his size, it was quite a thing to do and he actually could. These were not just stories because Smith didn't die until 1912. So there were people alive, when I was growing up, who still remembered Joe Smith. He could, they said, kick the ceiling with both feet. That was considered to be quite a feat. I don't imagine there's any competition in it today.

He was good on logs, on river drives. He certainly was respected because physical talent, physical might, was very much respected in the early wilderness where you had to survive. Things were tough and work was hard. People who did it well were looked at as kind of heroes.

Joe Smith, along with that, was a poet. A balladeer. He came back and married here and had children. He was always in fights and he partied all the time. He would steal animals for these parties. Crowds would have a night.

He was always playing tricks on people. Changing their gates, changing their animals from one barn to another. He seemed to have an obsession with tormenting people.

He would ridicule people in his poetry, write these strange things about them.

He understood the forest. He'd be away two or three weeks and would just lay down wherever he liked.

In one of his poems he mentioned something of the forest. He talked about, "The beasts of prey that hole by day and roam at will by night."

The woods is not Walt Disney at night. The woods is a lot like the jungle. As a young man I was lost for a night in the woods. The screeches of animals. Hawks killing weasels. Animals screeching out their last screech before they die. It's a very noisy, cruel place, the forest at night. He understood that.

He wrote a lot of satirical poems about a lumbering operation, a very poor operation and he worked there. One of the lines, he talked about the horses. Horses were supposed to be big and robust, if they were well-fed and looked after. In his line, he would slip these things in. He talked about, "The big red mare, her ribs shone bare."

The horses ribs were showing bare! It was an awful thing to say about this poor man who had this horse. A horse was very important and people who did that kind of thing would not be liked.

As I said, Joe used to steal and have these big meals and so on. He also stole to sell sheep, or whatever, to the bootleggers. A family, Conners, had their own still. In one of his lines he talks about stealing sheep. He says,

> Three dollars apiece without the fleece and money it was shy.
> Tomorrow we'll be rory-eyed drunk on Conners' rotten rye.

They would sell the sheep, $3 without the fleece.

One of his most interesting comments was probably with a neighbour of his, Dunc Munn, who invited him for supper. He knew that Dunc had stolen the sheep that he was eating but he didn't want to be too impolite about it. He was clever in how he said these things. Mrs. Munn invited him to eat and it was very common at that time to have the guest say grace. She asked him if he would say grace.

He wanted to make sure that Dunc understood that he knew where the sheep came from. He said,

God bless this meat that we do eat, Dunc Munn and I together.
God granted him speed that he did need to catch Mick Buggie's
wether.

A wether was a castrated sheep and he knew he had stolen Mick Buggie's sheep. This way, he got the message across.

Smith was up in the Central Lakes area trapping, in the late fall of 1912, with a couple of friends. He went across the lake and the other two people, fearing the ice, went around the lake. He went through with a bundle of traps on his back. Ninety pounds of traps on his back. He was a very strong swimmer. Had swum the rivers when the ice was going out in the spring. If nothing else, just to show he could do it.

He swam and broke ice. He came up twice and kept breaking ice. They said he broke up hundreds of feet of ice on the lake. When he came up the second time, he roared out to his friends on shore, "If I go down again, the devil can have me."

And he didn't come up. They found that his fingers were all broken up from beating the ice. He's buried in the small graveyard at Renous.

The end of Roving Joe, rogue poet of Renous River.

Another character was Dan McEvoy. He was a tall man, about six-foot-five. Very sharp wit and colourful language. He was fanatical about always telling the truth. He told things exactly as they were to people, in a pleasant manner but he told it exactly. That characteristic or quality of always telling the truth didn't endear him to his neighbours, who didn't always want to hear the truth.

One amusing incident with him. He was chasing a cow one day. His cow broke out. Back then there was herd law. There were pound keepers appointed in the communities. If your cow was out loose they would catch it, keep it and charge you. Animals couldn't run wild. I remember that, up until the '50s, the herd law was in effect here in New Brunswick.

In any case, Daniel chased this old cow. He'd say all kinds of kind things to the cow. He'd get up close enough to the cow and, just as he'd reach for it, the cow would take off again. This went on for an hour or two at least. He chased her for two or three miles. The cow would stop and the same thing would go again.

Finally, the last time she ran, when he was completely out of breath and he knew she was gone, it was no longer nice words. He roared to her. He said, "Go you speckled S.O.B. I hope I read in the *Family Herald* that you are impounded in Winnipeg for speeding."

Back then the only thing anyone read here, for the most part in rural areas, was the *Family Herald*.

An old friend of his who had been a very sinful person, if you wish, in the last years of his life got very religious. Dan, knowing this situation, he went to the wake. The lady, Mrs. Peterson, said, "My husband, Jack, he's in heaven looking down on us."

Dan was towering over poor little Mrs. Peterson. He looked down on her and said, "Mrs. Peterson, it says in the little red catechism, from hell there's no redemption."

He was not into hypocrisy, even at the wake.

Another case, even better known around our area, there was a family of Faders. They had eight sons. Lived away up at the head of the settlement. They lived a terrible rough existence. The eight sons never married and they fought and they drank and fought with everybody else. They went on this way for many years, to the point where there was no sanity or civility left in the home. Mrs. Fader had a very hard life, living with these eight sons and her husband. Finally she died and, as was the custom in those days, she was waked at the home.

Dan lived nearby. He went to the wake to pay his respects. When he went up to the coffin, Mrs. Tucker, who was a friend of Mrs. Fader's, said to him, "Oh Mr. McEvoy, surely Mrs. Fader is in heaven. She has suffered so."

Dan came back with, "Jesus, woman, even if she's in hell she's better off!"

So he wasn't going to be hypocritical under any circumstances. He was going to tell the truth.

I've one last character and I think this fellow is one of the most remarkable men I ever knew of, really, from the point of view of survival. The will to survive and being rugged. Not looking for anything from society. This man died probably twenty-five or thirty years ago. His name was Johnny Tucker. He had bad legs from a childhood disease, probably polio or something. He used to walk on crutches, in a circular manner. Powerful arms though and powerful shoulders. He worked in the woods, with these terribly bad legs and crutches.

He cut out things at home with axes. He made axe handles and peavey handles and sled runners. He was, in our area, the man to go to for that kind of thing.

He stayed at home, never married. Lived with his aged parents. He never looked for any free lunch from anyone.

He cursed and swore. He was very anti-religious. Life was a great fight for him, right from day one, and that's how he viewed it.

He wasn't an unpleasant man, although he quarelled with some people and he had very vicious enemies. And, of course, he also cursed these people. He was someone who gave no quarter but many people still enjoyed him and liked him.

In later life he lost the use of both legs and ended the last twenty-five years crawling on his hands and knees. He still continued to cut his own firewood, with bucksaws. He'd sit and saw the wood. He pushed it on little sleighs, on his hands and knees. He did this for years. Got wood to cut out for his axe handles.

He would bring in his own water. He shovelled his own driveway. He never looked for help from anyone.

After his parents died he continued to live alone. Some people were very cruel to him. He looked on them, of course, as great enemies. He had a terrible tongue for profanity and cursing them. He cursed the heavens. He cursed everybody.

The local parish priest, hoping to try to save his soul, went up to him sometime after the Second World War. He hoped to get an in with Johnny and he suggested to him perhaps that he could go to Ste. Anne de Beaupre. The good Ste. Anne might cure his legs. His only reply was, "It would be a wasted trip because, as St. Anne knows, if she ever cured me, the first thing I would do is kill three S.O.B.'s on Renous River!"

It was so characteristic. The priest, of course, went home, giving up any hope of saving Johnny's soul.

I mentioned South Esk and that's where we're headed next. Wonder where that name came from? Should have asked Ned Creamer after he finished telling stories. What stories he told!

Ned Creamer

I think it all started with my grandfather, by the same name, when I was just a child really, four or five years old. I was a listener first then, I guess, I was a storyteller.

I'll tell you a story that I haven't told many people but some of the older people knew. They used to say about the Creamers that their hair turned white very quickly. I didn't get this story from my grandfather directly but I got it from people that were pretty close to me, that were much older.

My grandfather was a teamster first and drove a team of horses and portaged stuff to people that were working in the woods. He was going to Holmes Lake. Today that's only about a three hour drive by car or truck, but then it was two days in and two days out. He was starting his second day, in the morning, about four o'clock and he could hear this screeching noise. He thought, "Well, I don't have to start yet. It's still dark."

The horses were in the hollow at that time. They were tied up and the wagon was there. He said, "I'll lie down for another hour. Get a little rest and then I'll start about 5:30, six o'clock."

When he did lie down, he could hear this screeching and he said this thing, an animal of some kind, dove over his head when he was kinda semi-conscious. The horses bolted and he was all alone forty-five or fifty miles from nowhere, to Newcastle.

When he did get straightened around and he got the horses levelled out the story goes, and I can remember grandfather's hair was pure white, he said it went pure white at the age of twenty-nine, because of the fright. The fright! And that was the story.

Supposedly, it was a mountain lion but this was a black one. I had no reason not to believe it and the Creamers had a tendency to that type of thing, to change their hair colour. My father was the same way. Not so suddenly!

There's the story of the big owl and he was big! He was just unreal. Jack, a friend of mine who's still alive, was a caretaker of one of the big lodges up here. He told the story.

"Yes," he said, "I saw the big owl. I was carrying a 300 Winchester Magnum and that's a pretty heavy rifle by standards today. That owl swooped down, up in Cains River there. Everything just turned dark. Almost like a great big 747 was passing."

He said, "I fired a shot at him. My 300 Magnum hit him somewhere in the head. All it did was knock a feather or two outta him! The owl still kept swooping. I figured, this is it! She's all over! Fired another one as he was going away from me. I'm a pretty good shot. I hit him again up there in the head area. Just knocked another feather out."

He said, "The story goes that he dropped down and, when he went to land, he tore up a stretch of ground, two or three acres. You can go up and see it there now!"

I went up and I said, "My God, that's where they're building the road. That's where they excavated."

"No, no," he said. "They didn't do any excavating. That's where that big owl set down. He was travelling!"

I said, "What do you mean travelling?"

"Well, he was going up to Montreal."

I said, "How do you know that?"

"He was in that direction. He stopped over in Fredericton. You remember, just a while ago, they had that flood there in that trailer park. He dropped down and ate two or three trailers!"

I said, "What?" And I just went along.

He said, "Yes. He ate a couple of trailers and kept on going. He never stopped again in New Brunswick. He couldn't make it all the way to Quebec City. He stopped in Drummondville. There was a great big salvage dealer outside of Drummondville and there was a lot of old engine blocks lying around. He dropped down and ate eight or ten engine blocks."

I said, "Holy dyin'. That'd be a pretty good feed!"

He said, "Yes, and that kept him going. The last we heard was that they wouldn't let him set down at Mirabel Airport, in Montreal. So he swept around there and, you heard about that devastation up there, just outside there? That wasn't a hurricane or anything like that. The big owl lost his bearings and he was losing steam. He dropped down there and he tore up quite a bunch of stuff in a suburb there."

And that was the end of the story. But this was Jack's story of the big owl.

When I heard this story first it was from a gentleman, he was a storyteller. He was talking about herding and he was stampeding and he was running cattle. Whatever. The story was that he was on a cattle drive and he said, "You know Ben Cartwright?"

And I said, "Yes. I've watched him on *Bonanza*."

"Oh yes," he said. "But I was with him!"

"Oh, you were?"

"Yes. And Doc Holliday. You know who Doc Holliday is?"

I said, "Well yes, I do have a little background on that."

He said, "Wyatt Earp and those?"

I said, "Yes."

This gentleman is gone now.

He said, "Well, I was on stampede with them and then I went on a drive with them. We took cattle from somewhere down in South America. We crossed the Amazon."

I said, "You did?"

He said, "Yes. We had 34,000 head of cattle."

I said, "That's a fairly decent herd of cattle. Yes."

He said, "We come across the Amazon. Oh, it was awful wicked. The water there, it's way wickeder than the Miramichi!"

I said, "Oh yes, it would be."

He said, "We crossed the Amazon and, when we come up through Alabama, our chaps were all froze. Everything was freezing on us. Then we crossed over and we went through the Black Forest!"

I said, "That's in Germany isn't it?"

"Yes. We went across quite a body of water."

I said, "Yes. You did so!"

He said, "We went into the Black Forest and all the trees there are black."

I said, "Is that right?"

"Yes, all the trees there are black. You don't know where we ended up?"

I said, "I have no idea!"

He said, "We went right down through the streets of Jerusalem!"

I said, "Of the 34,000, how many head was left?"

He said, "Oh, we didn't lose many."

And I heard that story over and over and over and over again, and very little variation, from the same individual. He was a real stampeder!

But all those were told in a kind of an atmosphere, you know, on the Miramichi.

This happened a few years ago. My cousin and her husband came down from Ottawa. He was with the bank. He's kinda retired now. Anyway, they came down and we had a cottage in Washburn Beach. Logieville.

I was going to university and I was trucking. That's how I paid my way through, handling pulp and working on a truck. We were, oh, just friggin' around, as they say here, one Saturday afternoon. It was a nice day, I said, "Why don't you come for a drive?"

He said, "Well, I'm gonna take my car. I'm not gonna drive with you. I'm a little leery. You drive too fast."

Well then, there wasn't very many cars. This was in the very late fifties, '59. I said, "We'll go up to Upper Blackville and go into the Cains River."

So we went and he had six pints of beer. Down here we didn't have pints. We only had quarts but they brought it down with them. We stopped up the road apiece and then went on. I said, "Just hold it. There's a lad stopped there at the side of the road."

This fella had his hand out. Greg wasn't gonna stop and I said, "Well, you have to stop in this part of the country."

Right in the woods. Right in the middle of nowhere.

This gentleman was there and he said, "H-how's she going today?"

And Greg just looked back at me. I was sitting in the back seat, his wife was sitting in the front. "What'd he say?"

I said, "How's she going today?"

Greg said, "Well, what am I supposed to say to him?"

I said, "Say, you're going the very best in the dear world!" This was a term we used, eh.

I jumped outta the back and stepped around. I was in really good shape. I was lifting right out straight then. He just looked at me. "H-how's she going now?"

I said, "She's going the best in the dear world!"

He said, "Who-o are yo-o-o?"

I said, "Well, does that make much difference, who I am? What are you looking for?"

He said, "Ga-a-hs."

Greg said, "He's gonna have to get it outta ours. I don't know how much gas there is. How far back is it?"

"We're about forty miles. That little car he's got's not gonna take very much gas."

And he had this glass gallon jug and a siphon hose. Everybody carried one of those. It was almost like your bank card or whatever, today. You carried one of those.

Anyway, the poor lad was down on his knees with this siphon hose into the tank, drawing on it, and the gas splashed all over his face and he was spitting and going on. And we had these cans of beer from Upper Canada. We were having a few tastes and they were calling me Ned. Ned this and Ned that.

"Wh-what's your name?"

I said, "Ned."

He said, "So-o is-s mine."

And I said, "Your name's Ned!"

"My name's Ned Peterson."

I said, "Yes, you are so."

He said, "Yo-o-o didn't offer me any beer, didja?"

I said, "No, I didn't but there's just a mouthful in this here, eh."

He said, "Well, that's okay."

He went over then to the little car. He had about a half a jug of gas. He went over to the little Metropolitan Nash, a little green one. I'll never forget it. His wife was in the car and a dog. Anyway, he went over and he said, "Do you see him? He's a wrassler."

He come over and he grabbed ahold of me. I figured, I should have known better up there. That's exactly what happens. When he grabbed me, I just went backwards and flipped him. Threw him about ten feet or so. It was an old gravel road, eh, and I jumped back on my feet and did a couple of handsprings, straightened out and pulled him back on his feet. He went over and said, "Didja see that! He can fly! He's dangerous!"

And then he come over and takes the dog out and says," You want me dog?"

This is how he was gonna repay me.

You know, I met him after. It's funny, he never forgot who I was and I didn't forget who he was either. I met him in town at Christmas. I was teaching recreational stuff over Christmas, still going to university. I was off during the dinner hour and I went downtown. He was wandering along. I stopped and got out and I said, "Hi. How are you, Ned?"

He said, "I didn't know you. How are you anyway?"

I said, "Oh, I'm the very best."

He said, "Would you like a feed a moose?"

I said, "Well, I don't know."

"Well," he said, "come on up."

I said I wouldn't get any time that day. Too busy.

He said, "Where can I get in touch with you?"

I gave him my number but I didn't figure he'd ever get back to me. And he didn't.

One time we were going along and I had this Charlie sitting in the truck. All of a sudden, this car went by me, just flying. There was a lot of gravel road there then. It kicked back this bunch of gravel and one piece struck right above where he was sitting. Hit the windshield. It was a company truck. Just bang! He looked over at me and he said, "I think he's got Firestone tires on!"

There's lots of bear stories. Years back, people used to have bears. They would get a young bear and let it grow up. It became a family pet. And these people here, they had a pet bear. He was just like a dog, like we have here. He was chained outside. They kept him outside.

The boys grew up and they got out having a few at night. One night they landed home, came into the yard, and the bear was loose.

Running around. This was about one o'clock in the morning. He said, "We gotta get this bear in. We have to put him in the barn. They left the bear out tonight and he's off the leash."

Silas said, "I'll grab ahold of him."

Silas was a big man. He was a pretty strong, able lad.

He said, "You open the barn door and I'll put him in."

They had big barrels in there. "We'll put him in the barrel until the morning."

They tore everything up, trying to get this bear cornered. It took about an hour to finally get him under control. Silas was all tore up and they tore up a lot of shrubs. However, they got the bear programmed. The other fella wasn't much help but they got the bear jammed down in and they got the top on the barrel. They went in the house. Silas hadda wash up, he was all bleeding. He just slept on the couch.

In the morning, Ed got up. The father. He went out about his chores in the barn. He come back in after a bit and he said to his wife, "There's two bears out there now, in the barn."

She said, "Oh, there can't be."

He said, "Oh yes. We have two bears!"

It was a wild bear that they hooked onto! It wasn't the pet!

In the same area, White Rapids and Grey Rapids, they used to talk about Ebenezer. How strong he was. They'd say, "Oh my God, Uncle Ebenezer's awful desperate strong! He was the strongest man that ever walked the Miramichi!"

I was all ears. About ten or so.

I'll just tell you how strong Ebenezer was. We hadda shingle the roof of the house and we didn't have any ladder. But there was a spur line, a rail line, that ran back about a half mile behind the house and it wasn't used anymore. So he went back and cut off about a hundred feet of this rail line, carried it out on his shoulder and laid it up against the house!

Somebody said, "Oh my God! He couldn't have lifted that! That'd weigh two or three thousand pounds!"

He didn't have a bit of trouble at all. He just walked right out through the woods with that on his back and set it up. And that wasn't the worst of it. When he went up to shingle the roof of the house, he was up there all alone. He was right at the peak of it. There was an awful severe pitch and he lost his footing. He started down and, just as he was goin' over the edge, he drove a spike in and he hooked onto it with his teeth. And he hollered *help! help! help!*

He was there for three days and he wore his teeth right out singing for help!

That's the way it was. Ebenezer.

Bill McKay, he was working up there in the woods. Friday night, the crowd all finished early and he hadda look after the teams and what have you. They hadda walk home and that was, coming down from Upper Blackville, through the woods and into Blackville proper. Anyway, he started walking. It was a moonlight night and he walked and he walked. Fifteen or twenty miles. He come to the top of this hill and he could see a silhouette. It looked like a horse in the offing. He thought, "That horse is out on the road. I'm gonna jump on his back and come right down to the Rapids."

He hadda come to Blackville, cross the Blackville Bridge and down the other side of the river to the Rapids.

He come up on it. It was getting dark. He jumped on the horse's back, grabbed what he thought was his mane, and the horse took off, wide open. Down the road, through the nine or ten miles of woods, just a blur. Through Blackville, across and out over towards Howard's. He said he hadda jump clear. He rolled right into the yard. He said he was gonna tie him up and he couldn't. He said, "You know what it was?"

Somebody said, "No. I have no idea."

"A bull moose! I jumped on a bull moose's back and come the distance!"

Oh, they told stories like that all the time and it was always kinda stretched. Just a little wee bit.

Heading back to Fredericton from Miramichi, we're going to make a stop in Stanley. When I went there to meet Sheelah Wagener, a fire engine led the way to a building right next door to her place. Fortunately, it turned out to be not too serious.

Sheelah Wagener

It was something that, like Topsy, just kinda growed. I have always enjoyed stories about the past, wherever I happened to live. And running this little inn in the middle of Stanley, I've found so many people who are interested in their roots and their past. They'll come back and maybe stay with me and maybe drop in because they're interested in the building because it's very old. And they'll tell me something that happened to their grandfather or a great-uncle. Then, if I hear a story that particularly takes my fancy, then I go to a lot of trouble to store it away in my memory and then I tell it to other people. And you often find it's a direct payback that you tell a good story and somebody tells you another one back.

This is one of my very favourite stories and I actually met this man, somewhere about 1991 or '92. He was eighty-nine at the time and he was seven when this particular adventure occurred. At that point, which is definitely pre-First World War, there was a small wood mill right at the bottom of Stanley Hill, where it intersects with the Nashwaak River. This man's father owned the mill. Presumably they had a little diversion of the water to make the water-wheel provide the power that drove the little mill. About seven or eight people would have been working in the mill and, indirectly, probably twenty or thirty cutting trees in the area around. So it was an important little enterprise for the village at that time.

This little fellow was seven and he was doing what seven-year-olds will, exactly what he'd been told not to. They had a millpond and the millpond had logs floating in it, waiting for their turn to be sawed up in the mill. He was riding around on a log with a piece of wood in his hand as a paddle. The millpond was probably seven or eight feet deep and it happened. He did fall off. Couldn't swim. It was pretty cold and he went down into the millpond.

Somebody inside the building looked out and noticed that the log on which he'd been splashing around was now empty and he was nowhere in sight. So this man raised the alarm and his father and all the other people working in the mill dashed out. Everyone of them got onto a log and each had a long pole. They were floating around on the millpond, feeling down into the murk with their long poles, hoping against hope that they might find the little fella before it was too late. They did find him, managed to hook his clothing with one of the long poles and they hauled him out. But, from their point of view, it was too late and he was dead.

They put the little body face down on the back of an old sloven which just happened to be there and was hitched up because it had just finished bringing a load in. The father, extremely distressed, left immediately, either riding a horse or driving a horse and trap, to go back up to the farm in Williamsburg to tell his wife and every other member of the family that they'd lost little Richard. Two of his men volunteered to drive the sloven to bring the little body home. And they were, of course, very distressed by the whole thing.

The sloven is a very rough conveyance and it was a rough time of year. They'd gone three or four miles and were approaching the driveway of the farmhouse where the family lived. There was a very big bump and rut and, as they drove this rough sloven across this bump and rut, it was a very big bounce. This threw the little corpse a few inches into the air. He landed on his front and it was sufficient to start the breathing process. He starts gagging and producing all this water that he's taken down into himself. Crying, obviously, because I imagine he was pretty terrified and the two fellas on the front of the sloven were absolutely petrified. Turned round and looked over their shoulders and saw this most unusual behaviour for a corpse. They then were elated and delighted and presumably banged his back and shook him round, put something round him and then drove up the driveway to the farmhouse.

And this eighty-nine-year-old, who's telling the story to me from his own seven-year-old memory, said it was the eeriest thing in the world — to come closer and closer to that house and hear the screams and roars of mournful despair from his mother and a couple of aunts who happened to be there, because they'd just been told, ten minutes earlier, that they'd lost their child. He heard it. Then they rode up to the door.

I can only imagine the wonderful reunion. Not many people get a second chance at life but that little fellow did.

This story was told to me by a wonderful, elderly gentleman. French and very courtly. Spoke very slowly but once he got going he was just marvellous. He'd moved into the area a few years earlier because his wife had passed away. He came to join a sister and a brother-in-law who had a farm on the Williamsburg Road.

He built himself a very small house behind the farm, on the edge of the woods because he liked his privacy. He described the house to me and he said, "Oh, it was just a wee little place." He said, "There were two little rooms downstairs. Two rooms upstairs. Then I just had a little lean-to kitchen. It was just a little slanty roof that was propped up by another little wall. It was just nice room for me and if one of my sons came to stay for the weekend, there was just about extra room enough for him."

He said that this particular year, by about the end of October or the beginning of November, it was beginning to get chilly. So he said, "I started making my preparations. Of course, I had got my wood. I'd felled it the year before and I yarded it out."

All these wonderful winter preparations. You did your own heating, completely, from start to finish.

"But," he said, "it was getting chilly. I thought, winter's coming. We're not going to avoid it."

The wind was quite strong so he said, "I got out the longjohns. I hung them on the clothesline which ran from my bedroom window out to a tree. There were three pairs and I thought it was a nice blowy day so they'd get nice and really well aired out."

"The next morning," he said, "I was getting up. I was in the bedroom and I saw movement outside."

Now, this was over the slanty roof to the lean-to kitchen.

And he said, "I looked out and, right on the other side of the glass, I'm looking straight at the face of the largest bear you ever saw in your life! And the bear was as startled to see me as I was to see him! I made a big jump and he made a big jump. He was obviously scared and he took off for the cover of the woods. Unfortunately for him, he got tangled up in my clothesline as he came off the slanty roof to my lean-to kitchen. He got tied up in the clothesline and in the longjohns. So that bear headed for the woods with one pair of my longjohns tied around his neck.

"You can just imagine, when I started telling my friends and neighbours. They all said it's going to be some bad winter, boy, if the bears are going to need the longjohns!"

These are what I call practical jokes and they're not all as funny as they probably set out to be. One that certainly isn't was told me by a man to whom it happened. He told me when he was in his eighties and I think this must have happened when he was in his thirties. It must have been shortly after the Second World War.

He told me that he was guiding some American sportsmen and they were in the wilderness between Stanley and Boiestown. These American sports would come up here and they liked their hunting. They also liked the good life that went along with it when they were having a week away from home.

The fella that told me this said, "We weren't going anywhere of an evening so they would do some pretty hard drinking. I must admit that I did my share along with them. They were very generous."

He said, "The previous day one of them had managed to get a moose. The evening was going well. It was very well-lubricated and no one was really feeling any pain. Somewhere along the line it occured to me that it would be funny to play a joke on them."

He said, "I can't imagine how I could ever have been this stupid. I went back behind the camp, where the carcass of the moose had been towed out to and was being dismembered. For reasons which I don't understand to this day, I picked up the moose antlers and I held them over my head. I came through the thicket, stamping as hard as I could, towards these sports that were all sitting around the fire well-lubricated."

And he said, "I need hardly tell you that that's the reason why I can't use my left arm properly! I was damned lucky that I wasn't killed for that piece of foolishness."

The next one is slightly less harmful. In fact, I think it's a charming practical joke. It's always amazed me, the number of churches in the area. I think any country area in the Maritimes has a large number of churches.

Anyway, there's one particular point about four miles from the village here, where we have two churches exactly across the road from each other. There's an Anglican church on one side, on the south side, and there's a United church on the north side. Between the two there's a distance of maybe twenty-four or twenty-five feet.

This particular fellow was walking home from a date. It was a beautiful summer's night. The moon was full, about one o'clock in the morning, and no one was around. Of course, back in those days, no one ever thought of locking a church. It still had the element of being a sanctuary.

Anyway, he was walking along and whistling. Said it was as light as day. And it struck him he'd always been intrigued that, in the middle of nowhere, these two churches were in such close proximity. So he thought, "I think I can get a big smile out of this."

He went into the United church and removed all their prayer books and hymn books. Carried them across to the Anglican. Collected the entire stock from the Anglican and carried them across to the United. Then spent ten minutes happily arranging them in all the pews exactly as they should be and then went on his merry way.

He heard rumblings of this afterwards but I often wondered to myself, what did they think? Did they think they'd got out of the car on the wrong side of the road?

He certainly couldn't ask!

The same fella told me another very short story which I think is very sweet. He said he was a great bird hunter. Most of the native game birds, their families and their generations and descendants, they all lived, always, within about two acres. They don't try and move around and conquer a territory twenty-five miles to the north or anything like that. So if you know of a good place for your partridge, you can usually go back fall after fall after fall and be fortunate.

Anyway, this fella had his own good place which was on the top of one of the hills around Stanley. It's the hills that make this village so attractive. He was up before dawn headed for this special place. There was a great big thicket and he just knew that the partridge were all in the area and, when the sun was up, they would come out and start trying to aquire their breakfast.

So he climbs into this thicket with his gun and he waits. He waits for about an hour and a half. Sure enough, he's lucky and out comes a partridge. He aims and fires. There's the partridge ready for him to sling over his shoulder and take home for supper that night.

As he's climbing out of the thicket to go and recover it, he thinks, "That's strange! This thicket is moving more than I would have imagined!"

And as he climbed out on one side, this very large bear is climbing out on the other side!

He said, "Going back and looking at it afterwards, we must have been less than two inches away from each other. Back to back! He didn't hear me climb in and I kept very still because I was waiting for the bird life. I don't know which one of us was more surprised but he got out and lumbered off in one direction. I didn't waste any time lumbering off in the other direction."

I just hope I manage to get this one right because the fella that told it to me was laughing so hard that he could hardly sit up. It must have been back during the '30s, I would imagine. Right up until quite recently, the men of the settlements would go into the lumber camps. In fact, I've been told that sometimes they didn't even get out for Christmas. They would actually go in and they would live in the camps for three, maybe four months. And there are wonderful stories that come out of those camps.

At any rate, two men were hired to man this camp. They were both hired with their vehicles. They would be driving sleighs or something.

One man had a horse who was a mare and was a pet. He just adored her.

The other one had a stallion. And the stallion would, naturally, take off in all directions if he got a mind to. So in order to find out where he was, he had a bell round his neck. Like a cow bell. So you always knew where this fella was. Every time he moved there would be this big clang.

At any rate, the stallion owner was feeling particularly mischievous at this stage. The owner of the mare had unharnessed her and was taking her down to give her a drink, some oats and rub her down. He was leading her down to the stream or the pond. The stallion owner, having penned up his beast, proceeded to take the bell off his neck, and wherever the poor man leading the mare was going, he was behind a tree within eight or ten feet letting this bell just ding gently. The mare owner was getting more and more frantic and saying, "Frank! Frank! Take that fella! Take him away from my beautiful mare!"

Anyway, I don't know how long it lasted but that story apparently reflected the kinds of things that they liked to pull on each other.

And talking about the lumber camps, I have this one from someone who cooked in the camps. Again, during the '30s and '40s. He told me that if somebody had a birthday, then it was up to the camp cook to do something a bit special and the men always appreciated it. Any little activity that made a change in their rather humdrum, everyday existence was appreciated.

This fellow said one of the people at the camp, there were probably fourteen or fifteen guys there, had a birthday. So he thought that when they'd all had their breakfast and gone off, and they wouldn't be back until supper time, that he would do something special.

"I decided to cook up cookies! I made molasses cookies and sugar cookies and oatmeal cookies. And when you're talking feeding men that are working outdoors in the winter, hard manual labour, you didn't estimate two cookies per person! You were probably going into double figures, minimum. Anyway, it was always good to have some around in a nice can for other times."

"So," he said, "I set out and I was making batches of cookie dough. Really large batches. I made six hundred cookies! Two hundred of each of the three kinds. I was just cooking in a shed they built to be my cook place. I didn't have counter space or anything so I set my cooling racks outside. I was just about to take out the last batch, maybe sixty or seventy-five, and I heard this mighty din from under the trees where I'd set out my cooling racks. When I looked out, here was Mister Bear and he was having the best birthday party of his entire life! I must have had five hundred-plus cookies outside and by the time he'd finished the ones that he ate, and I wasn't gonna argue with him, and the ones that he tipped on the ground and trod on, I might have had just over a hundred. No more than that.

This is a story that was told me by somebody who I just adored. She was a wonderful, wonderful story teller. Her name was Marg and I treasure her stories. They were simply wonderful.

She said that at one point when she was first married, which must have been probably in the 1940s, she and her husband were living in a very isolated place. There were only two families there. It was actually a little CN rail halt. Both the men worked for CN. So there was lots of isolation and they built their little house and they set up housekeeping.

It was a very beautiful place and still is. So they thought that they might as well build the outhouse on the bank of this slow moving creek.

On this particular occasion, it was in the middle of summer and it was just getting dark. Her husband was occupying the outhouse but, because there was only one family and they were about a mile-and-a-half away, he was occupying the building with the door wide open. So he could enjoy the sensation of watching the sun go down over this beautiful creek. The banks sloping down and the salmon jumping and everything was alright with the world. It was getting pretty dark at this stage and the moon hadn't quite come up. So it was very much the gloaming. Suddenly he heard footsteps. He quickly hauled himself up and put his head out to have a look.

He said, "I looked up and here's this fella coming down the path. I can't imagine what he was doing because he was wearing a black suit and he even had a white shirt. I thought, what is somebody doing coming down my path, towards my outhouse, so smartly dressed?"

Anyway, he said when he got just a few steps closer, he realized it wasn't a man in a black suit with a white shirt. It was, in fact, a large black bear with a white flash under his chin!

And he proceeds to amble past, totally ignoring the gentleman.

He said, "That can have quite an affect on you. At least I was in the right place!"

A ghost story! We bought a farm on the outskirts of Stanley somewhere in the middle 1970s, when it was my husband's ambition to keep all our children out of mischief by giving them so much to do that they didn't have the free time to get into mischief. So we had a lot of beef cattle on the farm and we looked after them ourselves. And our boys did all the haying, etc.

Anyway, it was a very, very old farm house. It had been built in 1852 and it had a great big, old woodshed behind it.

The story went that the original builder of the farm had had eight children. He had been an officer and had got this land grant by virtue of having fought, I presume, for the British government. Anyway, he had eight children. Four boys and four girls. Some of the descendants still live in the area to this day.

One of the boys, apparently, was not quite normal. He had some form of retardation. They found it very difficult to know what to do with him but eventually they discovered that he was very agile. Would have made a superlative gymnast in current times. But this was going back to probably the 1860s.

His name was Samuel and Samuel spent most of his time in the woodshed, which was two stories high and had big beams right across it. Apparently, people would come down just to watch him do these incredible tricks. He would do tumbling from the beams and it must have been close to sets of parallel bars. Things like that.

I don't think for an instant that the family kept him living out there. Just it was great amusement for him. At least they knew where he was.

When we owned this place, someone had told us this story. One day, when we were having a power failure, we were all sitting down there with just one small lantern. I decided to tell my family about this. Having two daughters with highly active imaginations, they proceeded to spend the night down there with their friends. And they were absolutely convinced that if you turned all the lights out and listened, you could in fact hear the movements out in the woodshed. You could hear the creaking of the beams as Samuel went through his ghostly tumbling act.

I didn't dare tell them, 'cause it would probably have scared them far more, that if there was anything out there moving around and there were noises from the woodshed, they were probably four-legged. Would have scared them far more than the idea of poor little, innocent Samuel doing his tumbling.

If you've been wondering when we're going to Prince Edward Island, wonder no more. Carol Kennedy in Charlottetown is our one and only storyteller from the Island, this trip. Maybe there'll be more in a second book.

Carol Kennedy

There's a house, perhaps no more than five minutes from Charlottetown, and I was going to show it to a local politician. He was looking for something a little private but not too private.

I arrived at this house first and thought I was in the wrong place because, until you're practically at the house itself, within fifty feet of the house, you don't even know it's there. It wasn't dark out, just sort of starting to dusk, I suppose.

I sell real estate for a living. Everybody makes fun of me because I don't like going to the back door. It's a thing with me. I think it dates back to my grandmother where, as children, we weren't allowed to use the front door. My grandmother, she's dead now, bless her soul, but she had some ways about her that I went the opposite way. When I was bringing up my children, we used the front door of the house. I always had the feeling, somehow, I wasn't good enough to go in the front door. I almost consider it an insult if someone says, "Let's use the back door." I use the front door! I'm fifty-eight years old. I'm still rebelling!

So up to the front door I went and I had the key. It was empty. I went to put the key in the lock and I just somehow couldn't do it. It was just a slight bit of discomfort.

Now this is a large, two-story house set in a grove of trees. It looks like something that you might see down in New Orleans, in

157

the bayou. It just had that look to it. A little scary but very pretty. Beautiful. The water behind it. A most beautiful water view.

I thought well, for once in my life, I'll go in the back door. So around I went and I opened the back door. Walked in the house just very slightly uneasy. Walked into a living room. The most beautiful living room I've ever seen in my whole life. It was panelled, but not the sort of panelling we think of. You know, if you see a British movie, you see this absolutely beautiful, very expensive panelling in libraries and things? That's what the living room was like. And a fireplace! The fireplace was three feet wide with lion heads on the end. So I'm fooling around with these lion heads, waiting. I'm uneasy and I don't know why.

I was really tempted to go upstairs because I had heard the bathroom was something special and I like bathrooms. So I started up the stairs. I didn't get very far. I put one foot on the step and I don't know how to explain it, I couldn't go any further. My other foot would not come up to the step. I could not move forward. And I put my hand up because it was like there was something there. But there wasn't!

I couldn't move. I just couldn't budge!

Nothing like that had ever happened to me before. Scared me.

I decided, the heck with this. Enough was enough and I got out of that house as fast as I could. I just ran!

And I waited for the gentleman I was showing the house. When he came in, we walked through the house. Whatever was there wasn't there. At least it didn't seem to mind so much when he was there, as it did when I was there alone.

Quite a few months later, I was telling somebody about the experience and they said that there was a ghost story connected with the house. That there was a girl who came down the stairs. Anybody who ever saw her, saw her on this staircase. She was quite pregnant and she had a sort of a Scottish band down across from her shoulder down to her hip and she would let out these mournful sounds.

I didn't hear anything but I sure felt something and I'm never going back into that house again. I don't like ghosts. They scare me.

In Summerside, we moved into a house. We weren't there very long when it was obvious that there was something going on in the house. It took quite awhile for us to figure out what it was. We finally did solve the mystery.

The ghost was a girl. She was a young girl and we called her Martha. At first, she didn't bother you too much. She didn't mind women but she didn't like men.

I remember one evening, my sister and I were getting ready to go to a street dance in Summerside, which was quite common a few years back. And Martha, I guess, decided to come with us! We were running up and down stairs, putting on makeup and things like that and I heard somebody running upstairs, laughing. Then running downstairs and laughing, with the click of high-heel shoes. I hollered up to my sister, "Don't wear high-heel shoes. We're going to a dance. Put on flat shoes."

She says, "Carol, I've got flat shoes on."

So I thought, "Oh great, Martha's coming to the dance!"

By then we'd been around Martha for awhile and, when we went to the dance, I wasn't very comfortable because I was never sure when I was going to turn around and bump into Martha.

She was odd. She would do cranky sorts of things. Like, if you were sitting reading with a lamp, the lamp would go off. Now at first, I'd shake the lamp, thinking there's something wrong with the darn lamp. But finally figured out, the only way to get the lamp on was to call for my mother. My mother would come in and she'd say, "Martha, turn that lamp back on." The lamp would come on! It would come on immediately!

If Mother wasn't home, you might as well go sit somewhere else. The lamp would not come on.

We had a grandfather clock on the second floor. One night we were watching television, a hockey game, and the clock started to bong, bong. You know, how clocks chime. We listened and then, suddenly, realized what was going on. We loved the clock but there were no insides to the clock! It couldn't go bong, bong. There was nothing there! Oh jeepers, Martha's at it again!

This was the sort of thing she did. She'd move furniture around. You'd walk into your room and the desk would be out from the wall. Just odd things.

I saw her once and that scared me. My mother saw her and my mother wasn't afraid of her. Mother related. In fact, Mother slept in the living room one evening, on purpose. She wanted to see Martha. On the dining room table was a tablecloth, a mirror and a bouquet of flowers on the mirror. Now every morning, you had to get up and replace the tablecloth. The mirror was there, the bouquet of flowers was there but every single morning the tablecloth was squashed up in a corner somewhere. It was every morning. You got into the habit. That was the first thing you did.

So Mother decided to sleep on the sofa because she could see the dining room from the sofa. She told me that she woke up. She had the feeling someone was peering very, very close down to her face. She opened her eyes and looked across the room and there was a young girl standing there. She wasn't the least bit nervous of it. Then she noticed that she could see the lamp, a floor lamp, right through the girl. She said that sort of startled her when she realized she could see right through her. Martha just sort of disappeared. Kind of just slowly faded. So that was Mother's experience with her.

My experience was one evening. My grandmother had sent me upstairs to get her sweater. I went up to the bedroom. The hall light was on. There weren't any lights on in the bedroom. I reached for the sweater on the chair, and I turned. And as I turned I just glanced out the window. There was a girl standing outside the window. She was looking out towards the back of the house. You could see the side of her. She was, oh, very pretty. Long, blondish hair, a white dress on. She looked quite normal. Then I realized that there wasn't anything out there. She's standing in mid-air. I figured, oh heck, and I stood there. Only my grandmother and I were in the house. I'm saying, "Grandma. Grandma." Of course she couldn't hear me. She's downstairs. And I didn't want Martha to hear me. I didn't want to move for fear that Martha would notice me moving. I didn't know what to do. Finally, I got enough nerve and I got to the stairs and yelled for my grandmother. My grandmother came up and looked out the window and she said, "Oh yeah, that's Martha." And she went back downstairs.

We moved out of that house because I don't like ghosts. I was at the point where I could only sleep in bed with all the lights on, my mother on one side of me and my sister on the other. I was an adult. I was in my twenties, for gosh sake. Nobody else was afraid of her, but she seemed to take delight, somehow, in startling me.

I'd walk around the corner and it was like someone was there. I'd jump right out of my skin. I can remember trying to bring my aunt through the kitchen door. We were walking into the kitchen. I walked in, my aunt couldn't go through the door. I tried to pull her, physically pull her, through the door and couldn't. She had to walk around through the diningroom and go in the other door to get to the kitchen.

One evening Martha threw an ashtray at my uncle's head. He had barely slid down into the bed and the ashtray crashed against the bed. A big, glass ashtray. Do you know, my uncle got out of bed and drove down to the ferry and waited all night for it. He wouldn't stay in the house another minute.

I think she's probably still there. What we figured out was Martha didn't seem completely sane. She'd laugh with this kind of a crazy laugh. It wasn't a normal laugh. Or sometimes she would just cry. You'd hear her and it would break your heart to hear her crying. It was like someone really broken-hearted. And she was quite young.

Martha showed up a few days after my grandmother and grandfather came for their first visit. On their way here, they had passed the asylum in New Brunswick. My grandfather had a sister. When she was about twelve years old, they put her in the asylum. I think, from the stories, probably the girl had epilepsy. But then they didn't know what it was and they put her in an asylum with a lot of people who were completely insane. Within a year she died.

Now my grandfather and grandmother were driving by and my grandfather told my grandmother the story. Then they came over to the Island. My grandfather's younger sister's name was Martha. We figure that Martha just got in the car and came with them.

So help me, it's all true.

We talk about it now, in the family, and we almost try to convince ourselves that we were imagining things. It's hard to believe, you know, that there really was a ghost.

I drive by the house but not any more than I have to. I go to Summerside quite often on business. But I don't want to get out of the car or anything because I don't want Martha to recognize me. I'm not bringing her home. No way!

Let's continue our adventure, along Nova Scotia's Parrsboro shore. We have a number of folks to drop in on and the first lives in Port Greville. Clayton Colpitts is retired now but still has a good sense of humour and a poetic way with words.

Clayton Colpitts

I grew up about five miles from here. I often think back. We hear these stories about the good old days. Well, I would say that was the good old days, according to the way the world is going today. In those days, we had very scarce living accommodations.

I don't know where, what place, I was born. It was back of Diligent River. I think probably I was born back on what they call Duffy Meadows. My dad must have met my mother when he was working on a log drive back on the Shulie River. She lived back that way. There was about 350 people lived back in this place that is nothing now but a forest. That's where I think that I must have been born. In those days, they used to live in log cabins and build camps and so on. They lived wherever they worked.

A Baptist minister asked me where I lived before I came here. I said, "Well, we moved every time the wind shifted."

Dad was a lumberman. He contracted milling and sawmills and so on. We moved from Ramsad River to Diligent River. From Diligent River to Parrsboro. From Parrsboro over to Point Wolfe, New Brunswick. From Point Wolfe up to Juniper, New Brunswick. Then back to Parrsboro again and then back to Diligent River.

We got married in 1940 and we moved to Port Greville. Been here ever since.

I worked for the government for twenty-one years. That's when I retired. I used to run heavy equipment, my wife taught school. So we bought this place.

I painted, off and on, all my life. I used to love to paint and draw. I've built furniture, I've built houses and I run heavy equipment. Also, I used to contract mills too, in my day, and worked in the shipyards down here.

See my shop out there? It's got a painting. That's a painting from Albert County, New Brunswick. The window in there is a covered bridge. You look in the window, you're going right in the covered bridge. I have a cottage out there and there's a painting on the front of it. There's one on the shed down here. I was the first one that ever did it around here.

I used to do a lot of cartoon work, mostly comedy. I would be working some place and something funny would happen, so I would draw a cartoon.

For instance, I was working with heavy equipment at Maritime Marshlands. One guy that worked there drove a float. He was unloading a dozer from a float up in back of Dorchester. Some way or other, the blade come down on his leg. Broke his leg. In the meantime, a Dutchman that was working with him got all excited and he fainted. This guy had his leg under the blade and he was shouting. A third fella took off up the hill to get a doctor, instead of him getting on the dozer and trying to lift the blade off. He was a dozer operator too. He got excited and away he went for a doctor.

Well, I drew this cartoon. The fella was in the Amherst hospital and his name was Art Stillman. So on the outside of the envelope I just put, "This parcel contains Art." And then I put "Stillman."

The cartoon showed this guy laying there with his leg under the dozer blade, his mouth open, and shouting. The Dutch fella was laying on the ground and a little bird singing above his head. The other fella was running up the hill, and kicking a rabbit outta the way to let a man run that could run!

That was the kind of cartoon I used to draw. I used to draw one pretty near every night I'd come home from work. Something would happen that I had a cartoon to take into the shop the next day.

Doc Black, an engineer, had a shotgun on the hood of his car so he could steer the car out on the marsh if he saw a pheasant or duck. When he got in line with them he pulled the trigger from inside.

I drew a cartoon of him when he joined Ducks Unlimited. There's a big lake and all the ducks flying over. In this cartoon, he had a bald head and Doc was walking down along the edge of the dyke, throwing feed out to the ducks. These two ducks flying overhead, one said to the other, "If it wasn't so embarrassing, I'd show you the wounds I got from that guy. Now he's down there feeding us!"

One guy that drove a dozer was Cyril Black, from Amherst. The dozers had no cabs over them and in those marshes, the flies and the heat out there in that hot sun, it just burned your flesh. So the drivers wanted cabs. They tried to get a cab on these tractors and the guy that was supervisor at that time, he was just so stubborn he wouldn't put one on. He just wanted them to know that he was supervisor and he was going to do what he wanted to do.

Finally, it got so bad, they had a meeting. Management eventually said they could put a cab on the dozers. The first day it was unfit to work on the marshes, raining or too wet, they were going to put these cabs on. The day came when it was a little wet. This fella took right into Amherst to get the welder and the material to get a cab welded on. This supervisor was away. Anyway, they put cabs on two dozers. They worked 'til ten o'clock that night to get the two of them on.

When the supervisor came back, it happened there was a call come in for the welder. They had to use it somewhere. Something was broken. He told the guy in charge of the welder, "I want you to load the welder and take it out."

He said, "Well, the welder's out on the marsh now."

"Out on the marsh! Where is it?"

"Out where I welded the cabs on those tractors."

He said, "You welded the cabs on! Who gave you orders?"

"They told me you said it was okay."

He sent him right out and they burnt the cabs off again! Took the blowtorch and burned them off again.

Anyway, I made this big cartoon. This guy used to go with his sleeves rolled up and was always smoking a cigar. I had this fella go-

ing on the dozer, the mud all plowing up, the smoke rolling out
from the cigar, and he was singing:

Old Mister Jonas, a very fine man,
He gave us a cab and a blower fan.
The sun can shine and the rain can pour,
I won't get wet nor hot no more."

I had that all done and I rolled it up and took it up to this engineer, Doc Black. He took it out to the supervisor. He said, "That's
one of them damn cartoons!" His wife got a great kick out of it.

I ran into a high powered line! We were on a marsh. Way out
on the marshes, there's no houses within miles. Never expected to
see power lines across there. This was down in Annapolis. The line
goes from the Granville Ferry side across to the other side at the
dykes. It's about a mile across. They have those high towers, a long
distance apart.

I had an oiler with me. I was running the drag line, moving
down the marsh about, oh, half a mile or more. They steer themselves you know; if you steer them straight, they'll go straight. I was
half asleep in the seat. It was plowing along about as fast as you
would walk. The oiler was about four hundred feet ahead of me. He
was walking along, smoking a pipe. All at once, the motor started
sputtering a little. I just got outta the seat and walked back to the
motor to see what was making it skip. When I got to it, it picked up
again, going okay. So I went back and set in the seat again. I looked
out and the boom seemed to be going up in the air. I looked again
and the smoke was flying outta the top of it. There was a five-
eighths cable and it was half burned in two.

Thirty-four condensers burned out in Annapolis. It shut everything off. But I was in the machine and it had so much iron on it
that it went right into the ground. I never felt it but the electrician
told me the next day, had I jumped, I never would have struck the
ground alive within twenty-one feet of the machine.

I ran into two or three different lines after that.

I had a close call, right off here, fishing one time. This place,
when we moved down here, you could go fishing and fill a boat in
one tide. You could swamp a boat with fish, they were so thick and
plentiful.

A fella and I took off one day, on the morning tide, in a boat that I wouldn't cross a millpond in today. We took it away out, fishing on the morning tide. We were gonna fish 'til the evening tide and then come in.

This Fundy shore here is very tricky. The wind can come up in a short time and boy, it can be very sloppy.

We were fishing away, catching so many fish we paid no attention to the wind coming up. We were bobbing up and down there, having a great time. Along about three o'clock in the afternoon, the boat was getting pretty well filled up with fish. The fella with me looked onshore and he says, "Boy, it looks pretty rough onshore. We better not fish anymore."

It was a little early to get in around the pier down here; however, we started for shore. One fella was to row awhile and then the other guy. In the meantime, he went to pull the anchor in. It caught. It wouldn't let go of the bottom and it almost swamped the boat there. Just took in a little water. Pulled the bow down. I said, "My gosh, no! Cut the rope! Cut it. Don't pull it." Just then, the anchor let go and he got the anchor in.

The fish was just swamping back and forth. He was sitting in the stern and I was doing the rowing. We darsn't change. We darsn't move around. The closer to shore we got, the rougher it got. We had probably a hundred yards to go to get down to the pier and it took us about an hour and a half to get down that far. The wind was against us, the tide was against us. We darsn't come ashore. If we came ashore we'd be sure to be swamped 'cause the waves were about eight and ten feet high. So I kept rowing 'til I got down to this pier. We figured we could get in back but when we got down there, the tide wasn't in far enough to get into the pier. I kept holding my own until my hands were so blistered I said, "It's one thing or the other. We got to give up or do what we can."

He said, "Steer it for shore. Try and keep it stern to the waves."

So I started. Kept it to the waves alright! The first wave carried us right up back of the pier. Alright as far as that goes, but before we can get on our feet we were hauled out again. The second time, a wave came right over the boat but it brought us both onshore. This other guy was across the boat, hanging on. I jumped. When I jumped onshore, I had a hard job to hold my footing because the gravel was rolling underneath. I jumped and I had the anchor line around my body. I got ahold of the rope and, when the boat came in the next time, I held it. It almost pulled me in but I held it. So he got out. He was just about all in and so was I.

We had a boat full of fish. We just let them go.

I'll tell you a story that's kind of humorous. This old fella used to work with my dad. His name was MacDonald. Angus MacDonald. He had an old horse and wherever you would see Angus, you'd see this horse. I guess Angus must have followed my dad around for about twenty years, as far as I can remember, from one mill to the other. He had this old horse and they'd have him hauling wood out from the mill or hauling water in. Doing chores around like that. He wasn't a very strong man.

He lived in Parrsboro, not too far from where we lived. So one day, Angus was walking in town. A neighbour said, "Where's your horse, Angus? You're always driving your horse."

He said, "Oh, the horse got sick."

Angus didn't talk any longer and, about a week or two after that, this same guy had a horse and it was sick. He called Angus and asked what he gave his horse when it was sick. He said, "I gave it a quart of turpentine."

"A quart of turpentine?"

"Yup. Raw turpentine."

So, about a week or so after that, he met Angus again in Parrsboro. He said, "Angus, I gave my horse turpentine. You told me you gave yours turpentine."

"Yup," he said.

"I gave it to the horse and it killed it!"

"Yup. Killed mine too!" Angus said.

This poem is called "Dad."

> The old man sat in his rocking chair, his body was frail and old.
> His face was a page in history from the stories he had told.
> His younger days of long ago, he wasn't the type to shirk.
> He'd take his turn, he'd never shirk, he was never afraid of work.
>
> He worked in the lumber woods, at farming gave a hand.
> He laboured in the shipyards and sailed to many foreign lands.
> He struggled hard to make ends meet,
>   he lost a dear, young wife.
> He'd left four children in his care, to occupy his life.

But he struggled on, he laboured long, he put his trust in faith.
He trusted God to give him strength.
That God would him embrace.
He could tell you things that happened,
      near a hundred years ago.
He could keep you spellbound, listening.
Stories of things you'd like to know.

For seven years he struggled on, no wife to share his home.
A little family to feed and clothe and do it all alone.
And then one day, perhaps by faith, a little later on in life
He met a fair young lady, to become his second wife.

Three more children blessed their home and added to the fold.
The only regrets he had, he said, that he was getting old.
For almost one hundred years he had toiled
      and worked the land.
He always claimed that God was there, to lend a helping hand.

And now at last, his mind alert but his body lame and spent,
He was ready to meet his Master and that's the way he went.
He suffered not when he lay down, he just lay down to sleep.
And now, God has him in His care and forever will He keep.

That was my wife's dad.

I've written poetry most of my life. Some of these poems are from way back. Here's a little short one, "The Master's Plan."

When God made the world He skillfully planned
Beautiful mountains and rivers and trees.
Created animals and beautiful birds,
Created the tiny wee bee.

He made the sun to rise and shine,
He gave us moonlit nights.
He gave us hills that we could climb
To view the worldly sights.

He made the little birds to sing,
Perfumed the little flowers
So we could live in harmony.
Yes, all of these was ours.

After creating all these things
He set the world agog.
He gave to us the pleasure
Of a boy and his little dog.

Sometimes a thought would strike me. This just came to me as quick as that.

The Frog and the Toad

A proud little frog sat sunning himself beside a country road.
Without a warning, was accompanied by a scrawny-looking
    toad.
Now, the toad seemed quite contented
    and settled down to rest
But the frog was very unhappy with his uninvited guest.

"You see Mister Toad, if you don't mind, I'd like to say alas.
Just go hopping down the road
    and meet someone more your class.
You see, we frogs are very proud. We choose our company well.
We like to dress with dignity. In popularity, we are swell."

"You see, Mister Toad, your dress is drab,
    warts all over your back.
We frogs rank high in fashion, we have lots of things you lack.
For instance, I have a wonderful song
    I can both whistle and sing.
For you toads, for quality and such, I just can't think of a thing."

"I can swell up like a big balloon
    and catch flies with a flick of my tongue.
Now, if you don't mind, go hopping along
    and I'll finish my rest in the sun.
Another thing I can do better than you,
    I can hop a lot farther, by far.
I'll give you a sample. I'll show you right now." He hopped right
    out in front of a car!

Now the toad to himself said, "There's things I may lack,"
As he went hopping along down the way.
"But I don't have tire marks over my back
And I'm enjoying the sun of the day."

Now, the moral of this story shows that boasting doesn't pay.
Had the little frog been like the toad,
    he'd have lived another day.

This is "The Shipbuilders."

Come you folks and listen, a story I will tell.
I worked with this crew and knew them all well.
We had to build ships to win this great war.
Some of our young men had gone on before.

There were Hatfields, MacGillivarys, McWhirters and Grahams.
MacAloneys, McCulleys, from all walks they came.
There were caulkers, mechanics and blacksmiths there too.
There were millmen, surveyors, that made up the crew.

Ross Graham was the planker, ambitious and keen.
On a cold, frosty morning, you couldn't see him for steam.
Says, "Come now you fellows, pull up your pants.
Let's get the thing ready and send her to France."

With clanging of clamps and mauls ringing out,
"By gary that's good," you'd then hear them shout.
And Clayton Spicer, from away down the shore,
A famous wood planer, he's slow but he's sure.
Always remember, this was his text:
"If she's not ready for this war, she'll be ready for the next."

Then there's George Wagstaff, with his keen eye.
If your work didn't suit him, he'd bid you goodbye.
John Kerr and his horse was always about
Hauling a plank in or hauling one out.

Fred Hatfield, the tallyman, with a book at the door,
Marked every piece down that went through the door.
If a piece was brought out and re-sawed in the mill
'Twould be measured again and marked on the bill.

Then Otto, by gosh, who owned a big share,
Was interested in fish, for war didn't care.
If the herring was running he'd go for his net.
His supply of cod for winter he'd now have to get.

170

There was Dave with his auger and Russ with his crew.
Beat them at their game, you've got something to do.
Now when she's all planked and the decks are all laid,
The smoothing, with planers, will now have to be made.

With chaws of tobacco all stuffed in their face,
The shavings will be flying all over the place.
They plane and they chaw, they spit out the juice.
You'd think that Niagara had just been turned loose.

And now Dick McLellan, a painter by trade,
With battleship gray he'll give her the shade.
There's Don Lake the millman and Don Lake the clerk
And Charles Murphy, the foreman, to keep them at work.

Oh yes, there's Harris Thorpe, ho, ho, by jove.
He's from Hall's Harbour, way up the cove.
Then there's Winters, there's Crossman, Allens and more.
They're all shipworkers from Parrsboro shore.

Now, if Adolph Hitler is a bit smart at all,
His armies and battleships he will recall.
When he takes a look out over the Rhine
And sees these ships coming, all in a line,
He'll probably break down and his blood it will chill
When he spies the armada from the Port of Greville.

We're in Parrsboro now and I have to tell you a secret. I think I can get away with it because I'm no longer on CBC radio. If you listened to my show, you might remember I'd sometimes talk of my "nameless friend" in that town. Nameless because she didn't want me to mention her name on the air, because somebody was sure to stop her on the street and talk about whatever I had said relating to her. So my friend since my early teens, Ann Davison (nee Tupper), thanks for talking sense to me sometimes and thanks for putting us on to some of the storytellers along your shore. Now let's get down to the docks for our meeting with Conrad Byers.

Conrad Byers

Parrsboro is certainly an historical town, but I think the main thing was when I was growing up all my neighbours were older people. Retired sea captains. Growing up on the side of the harbour, I took an early interest in shipping and hearing all the stories of the sea. I was just always interested in that. Even when I went to university, I took history. It's just part of my life.

This is a true account of a local man. George Hatfield was his name. He was born in Port Greville and lived in Parrsboro. It was on a barque called the *J.T. Smith*. This would be 1874. The vessel had left in March of that year. They'd gone down to Cuba for sugar and left there for New York. It wasn't hurricane season but it was quite rough weather when they left. The captain had been on his feet for a couple of days. And the crew. After a couple of days the weather started to moderate a bit so he saw his opportunity to get some sleep. He went below. Still had his clothes on in case he was called in a hurry. He just got to sleep when someone tapped him on the shoulder and said, "Let her fall off a half a point."

The term half a point, by the way, is a sailing term. The compass rose is divided into points. I think it's eleven and a quarter degrees. One point. So it was quite a few degrees of the compass to change course.

Anyway, Hatfield thought the mate had come down, or whatever. So he got up and went up to the mate. He said, "I already gave you the course. Why'd you wake me up?"

The mate said, "Nobody was down. I'm still on the course you gave me."

So he went down below, kind of embarrassed. He goes back to sleep again and just gets to sleep, when the hand's on the shoulder again with the tap. "Let her fall off a half a point."

This time he came up and bawls the mate out for disturbing him and said, "I gave you the course and don't wake me again!"

The mate said, "Nobody was down below."

He goes down again and eventually, while he's thinking about this, he falls asleep. The next time the tap comes on the shoulder, he wakes right up and sits up. It's not a request this time. It's a demand. This man says, "Let her off half a point!"

So he sits up and he sees the man! Watches the man turn and walk up the companionway. Up the steps. Notices his clothes and so on. He realizes it's nobody aboard his ship.

He comes up to the mate and says, "Did you see somebody walking up by?"

"No. Nobody came up."

They search the ship and they don't find anybody.

He thought, maybe a stowaway or something. He goes to the mate, 'course they all think he's crazy, and says, "Okay, let her off a half a point." Then he goes below and goes to sleep and sleeps soundly the rest of the night.

Hatfield gets up in the morning, comes up, and he thought maybe he'd dreamt the whole thing. He looks at the compass and, sure enough, the mate steered on the second course. He orders a sharp lookout and soon somebody says, "A lighthouse on the horizon!"

Of course, they were way out at sea. There can't be a lighthouse. So he gets the binoculars on it and they see it's a vessel in distress. The masts all twisted and everything. It's an American schooner in distress and sinking. They send their boat over and it takes a couple of trips to get all the crew off. They just get the crew off and the vessel sinks. The captain of the American vessel, the *Talbot*, was a Captain Annsbury. He had his wife and child aboard.

Once they were rescued they said, "Why are you way out here? Because we were blown way off the trade winds, the normal sailing routes to New York. We never thought we'd be rescued."

The captain related the story and what he thought was a dream. Captain Annsbury's wife asked what this man looked like. The captain described him, his clothing and everything. She looked at him and she went pale. She said, "That's a perfect description of my father, who died at sea ten years ago."

Hatfield took the people ashore in New York, and President Grant, of the United States, presented him with a gold watch and chain. For courage and valour for saving American citizens. The family still has it in their possession.

Three years later, there's another little add to the story. Captain Hatfield and his wife, Mary, had a son which they named Annsbury Hatfield. After the captain they'd saved.

He went to sea many years after that and didn't have any other touches with the supernatural. He died in Amherst, at ninety-one. Almost fifty-four years to the day of that occurence.

There's kind of a ghostly story, in a sense, with another vessel from the Parrsboro shore here, the *Cumberland Queen*. She was a four-masted schooner, built about 1920-21 in Diligent River. She had a very strange experience. She was coming up from Turk's Island in 1922 with a load of salt. They used to go down there for salt for the fishery. This would be in May of '22.

She got in a storm off of Cape Hatteras, a very dangerous area with all the sandbars and very steep seas in a wind storm. One of the planks started to open and she was taking water. The end result was that she was sinking. The crew abandoned her and they were later rescued, but the vessel sank.

The next March there were some fishermen out in the area fishing, and suddenly the vessel came up out of the water again!

She'd dissolved all the salt out of her hold and came up. She still had the tatters of sails on her.

Imagine, seeing those masts come up out of the water!

Anyway, they put a line aboard her and towed her into Norfolk, Virginia. There were just minor repairs to fix the plank and re-caulk her. She sailed for another thirty years after that.

One of the more famous capsizings involved a three-masted schooner built in Port Greville in 1904, the *Sekata*. She was lost down in the Gulf of Mexico. It was an odd thing because she was sailing along in relatively light winds. It was raining a bit but not a squall or anything. Suddenly the mate saw kind of a catpaw of wind coming. He yelled to the captain at the wheel to put the vessel up into the wind. There was a gust coming.

The captain either panicked or, being his first command, he didn't bring it into the wind fast enough. 'Course, everything was caught and she just capsized before they could do anything.

As the vessel heeled over, the men tried to climb up on the rigging, as it went on its side. When it went completely upside down, they tried to climb up onto the hull. Only one man, the mate, succeeded. The rest were hanging on the side. Everyone except the man on the hull was drowned.

There is a letter that he wrote home to the family, when he got into Florida, explaining what happened. I'd just like to read that because it's really to the point.

> December 9th, 1905, Port Tampa.
>
> With bitter pain and sorrow I write you this letter of the wreck of the schooner, *Sekata* and loss of her crew. We were running before heavy seas and wind on Thursday, 19th December. It was raining heavy at the time, about ten a.m. We were engaged filling water tanks, captain at the wheel.
>
> I saw a shift of wind coming and called to the captain. I spoke again to him and ran to the spanker tackle as the sails took aback. I got it over alright and run to the other sails, calling the watch at the same time. The vessel was heeling down. I let run the peaks and sheets but it was too late. It was over too far to right. When the water was on the lee rail I called to all hands to save themselves and jumped on the bulwarks. The captain run to the mizzen rigging, Mr. Collin to the fore. Stewart with me and two sailors in the main. We all tried for the keel but I alone reached it, just as she went bottom up.
>
> In two minutes, four men, the captain, cook and two seamen, came on the surface on pieces of

wood. But Mr. Collin came up too and, I saw, with one seamen. For five minutes they kept by the vessel then the heavy seas swept them astern. Only one man, a sailor, was drowned alongside. I saw the cook, the captain and one sailor then half a mile astern. To my dying hour the sight will be with me.

I tried, by tying my clothes together at first, to reach them. There's not a rope nor stick that I see and I could not reach them. Frantic with grief, they were washed astern away from me and I was left alone.

Oh God, how hard it seemed. No man, who has not seen this sight, can think or realize it. In four days I was alone, constantly wet by seas, without a bite or a drink. But I did not mind that as the terrible feeling of lonesomeness. Not a sail or a moving thing.

But I will not dwell on myself for I was saved and am quite well. I was taken off by the four-masted schooner, *Helen Thomas*, and treated in the very best way and landed at Tampa. I had to take off my clothes to swim to the boat as they could not come near the wreck.

The consul has given me a passage to New York where I leave for tomorrow. The *Sekata* lies abut sixty miles from San Blais. Hull alright, spanker out over the side, all washed and torn. Cannot be towed in except the masts should happen to get out. She lies in deep water.

Give my heartfelt sympathy to Mrs. Captain Collin. May God help her as He did me.

Yours truly, J.B. Williams.

They were known as letters in black and they really were. There was special stationary you could get to tell bad news. This one here, the original, was outlined or margined in black and the envelope had black corners. So you knew when you were getting bad news.

There was another vessel built in Parrsboro called the *Enterprise*. She was a small schooner. She had the distinction of capsizing on three different occasions and drowning the crew. The last time that she was lost the owners wouldn't even claim her. She was just capsized on the shore and they said, "We've lost too many men and we don't want her." The captain of the tugboat that hauled her off took her and no one would sail her again. So they took the masts out of her and they used her as a water boat, to take water out to the freighters and the square rigged ships that anchored at West Bay and loaded lumber. She was in that trade for a few years. Eventually she just went to pieces. She had drowned quite a few people.

I think that it's maybe a characteristic of many rural areas but certainly we in the Maritimes, I'm told, have the habit of never answering a question directly. We always tell a story to illustrate the point, or whatever. That, I found, can be annoying to some people outside the area.

I used to do a bit of sailing. One time I was helping an American who had bought a Nova Scotia schooner that was built here in Parrsboro. I was helping him sail it south, with a friend from here.

My friend and I would always be telling stories at the wheel. Yarns about this and that. The American crew would just kind of shake their heads. They'd ask us a question, "Well, where did you learn that?" Or, "How do you do this?"

We wouldn't say, "Well you do this, or so and so taught us this."

We'd have this big story about it. It got so they'd just shake their heads. You know? They thought maybe it was just the two of us that were a bit strange.

Later on in the voyage, I had another friend of mine from Nova Scotia come down when we were in the Bahamas. Invited him aboard and we decided to sail over to Florida. When I was below I heard my friend up talking to the captain at the wheel. I could hear the talking going on. Meanwhile, in the next cabin to me are the other American sailors and I heard one of them say to the other fella, "My God, it's true! All those Bluenosers are the same!"

177

The next spot on the Parrsboro shore we're visiting is Ward's Brook. I know, I seem to be taking you back and forth along this road but it's such a pretty drive, from both directions. Just feel all that fresh air coming in off the water!

Jessie McCully

My grandmother on my father's side, that would be my paternal grandmother, she was born in 1841 in Douglastown, New Brunswick. When she was thirteen years old they left New Brunswick and came to Nova Scotia. They came by train to Parrsboro and then they had to pack horse through the woods to get to Port Greville. That's all I know about it. They came because of the shipbuilding. All that family, they were shipbuilders.

Some of the people of Cumberland County came from the state of Maine, the ones who were in favour of Britain. The ones who weren't in favour stayed in Maine, of course. But the ones who came here were afraid also of the border raids by the Fenians. They trained some troops down the shore. I know my grandfather, on my paternal side, trained down at Grant's field. He got $200 in gold for training. But he didn't leave any of it to me.

When I was three years old, I remember Mother had a birthday party for me. All the little boys and girls from the place were there. Two of the boys, from the same family, they gave me the same kind of gift — a little white pitcher, like you used to get in a restaurant. I married one of the boys. Not at three years old though.

About 1930, somewhere around there, he walked home with me from a dance. Then he walked home with me every night afterwards, I guess. We courted a long time. We walked and played games. No snakes and ladders. One woman said she played snakes and ladders with her man but I didn't believe that.

When I was teaching school, we were having a geography lesson. This was in Lakelands, above Parrsboro. The question I asked the kids was supposed to have been, what are the four parts of Russia? I made a mistake and said, the four farts of Russia. When I got home to my boarding house that night I said to the boarding mistress, "I made a mistake at school today."

And I had to tell them what I had done. It was the Jeffers family and he was a great guy to laugh. I told him, "I asked the kids what were the four farts of Russia?"

Very straight-faced, he piped up, "Stalin! Who were the other three?"

I was teaching in Spencer's Island and I liked it there. They were very nice to me. The secretary had offered me a raise for the next year, if I stayed. But my parents went to Pictou. The war was on and my boyfriend went to Pictou. And I was bound for Pictou! So I left at Christmas time with the idea that, if they didn't get a teacher to take my place, I would come back. The sixteenth of March I went to work at the Royal Bank of Canada in Pictou. I liked it there. I loved it. Then the war ended and we were off to someplace else.

I've had a car for years. I like to drive. I had an accident not too long ago. I was travelling down from Parrsboro one afternoon. There was a man in the front seat with me. Wasn't my boyfriend. He travels with me on Fridays to get his groceries. There was a woman in the back seat too.

We were coming down through Diligent River and I said, "We don't have to go too fast. We've got all the afternoon to spend."

So we got to the Fox River bridge and there was a pheasant in the road. Not in the road, on the side. Right on the curve but this side of the bridge, thank God. I didn't want to run over the pheasant, so I slowed down and I kept going around the curve. The pheasant was walking along side of me. I couldn't get clear of the thing.

And the man said to me, "Oh Jessie. Watch out!"

I was headed for the ditch! The ditch was as steep as this ceiling. Eight feet probably. I had sense enough to try to steer down the ditch. You see, I thought if it went head first would be easier than going sideways. The tire came off the wheel and I guess that pushed us down sidewise. We landed on our top.

Well, that wasn't too good. I have a breathing problem and I couldn't breathe. I had to get the windows open as fast as I could. I got the windows open first and then I got my seatbelt off. I turned the car off, then I decided I must get out of here. By that time our rescuers were taking the man out. He was yelling, "Cut the seatbelt off! Cut the seatbelt off!" He had broken his arm.

I looked out first and the reeds were sticking up past the window because I was in the roof of the car. I thought, "Oh, the snakes and the bugs and the toads and everything. I can't go out through there."

Anyway, I ventured and some guy was out there from down shore. He took me by the hands and helped me. I lay there for a little while, tried to breathe. Finally, they put me in the ambulance and gave me some oxygen.

The lady, she didn't have her seatbelt on so she got out quite easily.

When I went to reinsure my car that fall, I couldn't get an insurance company. They weren't gonna insure me. They said I'd had two accidents. I don't know where but I must have had two accidents they knew about. They charged me $1,200 more insurance a year than I had been paying. I was paying $800. So that's the end of that story. But I still have my car and I still have insurance.

We used to try to smoke cigarettes. We'd stop after school and get the dry snake breaks. You know, the old dried ferns. Break them up and we'd find a piece of paper on the side of the road. What got me, we never knew what was in the paper. They tasted alright. We were making smoke. That's about all we were doing.

Then we used to go to C.G.I.T (Canadian Girls in Training) and we made baskets. There was a kind of reed that we used for the baskets. We smoked them once in awhile too.

I didn't really smoke then. I didn't smoke until 1934, I think, and then not much. But later, a lot. I quit one afternoon, the week that my father died.

My dad was always at me, "Jess, you better stop smoking." He'd smoked for years and he quit right off. He said, "You better quit smoking. It's no good."

I went up to see him at the hospital on a Tuesday. We talked. Then, when I come out, I lit a cigarette and I said to the girl who took me up, "I'm not smoking another cigarette." And I threw it out on the street. I've never smoked another one since.

I went up on Thursday to see my dad and he was in a coma and couldn't talk to me. So I didn't have the pleasure of telling him that I had dropped my cigarettes.

Grandfather Ayer worked on the ships, same as all the Ayer boys. This was a ship from the West Indies and one of the crew members gave him these five little stones. There were more. Mother must have given some away. But I have five of those little stones. You put them in your eye and they will take out any dirt that can be taken out of your eye. I've had one in my eye and it made my eye feel better after it got the dirt out.

They're older than I am. Now this is my grandfather's home and I've been here seventy years. Long before that they were given to him. I keep them in a little Dodd's Kidney Pills box and the brown sugar feeds them. They're really little crustaceans and that's their feed, as far as I know.

If you put them in vinegar, like that, they'll move. There!

There it goes! The big one moved. You see the bubbles coming? One fella's on his belly or upside down. They don't move around and around, they'll just dart, like. I wouldn't be surprised water'd do the same thing, make the eye stones move. They're getting going now. You can judge whether they're alive or dead. They probably enjoy getting out for a little run.

Back towards Parrsboro again. You can see Cape Split and Cape Blomidon way across the Minas Channel. This will be our first and only visit where we'll hear a war story, among others. Our host is Clayton Graham of Diligent River.

Clayton Graham

This is a ghost story that was told to me many times, ever since I was a young boy, about Stoney Hollow. It's a little side road going down to the wharf. It seems that, at one time, there used to be a peddler coming around. This peddler was a short fellow and he always wore a dark suit. Somebody murdered him, right at Stoney Hollow. Apparently they murdered him with an axe and cut his head off. Different people said that they used to see this little fellow walking at night or early in the morning and he didn't have any head.

There was a gentleman here who used to haul lumber from the sawmill down to the wharf. He used to load up at night and leave early in the morning. This was the fall of the year and it was practically dark when he left. He wanted to get so many turns in with his team of horses.

It was coming daylight as he approached Stoney Hollow and he was sitting on the wagon about half asleep. All of a sudden, as they dipped down into the hollow, the horses reared up and stopped. Put the brakes right on and give a startled snort out of them! The poor old fellow, he sat up. "What the heck's going on?"

He looks ahead and there's this little man standing in the middle of the road. The horses refused to go. The little man walked right up in between the horses. He jumped up on the pole between the horses and he walked straight back towards the driver!

The driver was sitting there, just shaking. He was paralyzed. He couldn't move. He didn't know what to do.

As the little fellow got right back to where he was, he turned to the left, jumped off and ran into the woods.

He said, "I swear to goodness, he didn't have a head!"

Later on, as he was visiting one of the neighbours, a fella asked him, "Did you ever hear the story about the ghost in Stoney Hollow?"

He said, "Oh yes. I've heard it several times."

"Well, a neighbour of mine that lives down the shore was here one night. We were telling the ghost stories and 'course this one came up. It was dark and I said to him, 'You're walking home are you?'

"He said, 'Yes. I want you to come down early in the morning and we'll go fishing.'

"So he said to his neighbour, 'I bet you won't go down by Stoney Hollow tonight.'

"Oh yes, I will," he said. "Yes, I will."

"You prove it to me. You get along there, you cut a little alder and lay it across the road. Right there at Stoney Hollow. I'll be down in the morning and I want to see that alder across the road to prove you went that way instead of going around the long way."

So the next morning, as he approached Stoney Hollow, there was a little alder across the road. So he thought, "I guess my friend walked this way last night."

Just then he heard footsteps coming and he said, "I sort of bristled up. It was a little foggy and I could see a little fellow coming along the side of the road. I thought, if my friend walked there last night, I'm gonna stiffen right up and I'll just get over to the side of the road, as far as I can, and I'll walk by him. Just as he come abreast the fella said, 'Hello Russell!' I must have jumped two feet in the air!"

Then he said, "I recognized the voice. It was a neighbour of mine."

And that's the ghost story.

In 1939, war broke out and I was just at the age, really. 1940, I was twenty-one years old. I was called up for military training for thirty days. Anyone that was twenty-one and physically fit, it was compulsory training for thirty days. I took that training in Stellarton, here in Nova Scotia. At that time I used to listen to the radio. How things were going over in England, you know. The blitz was on there and it appeared to me that they really needed pilots. I was quite interested in how the British pilots were coping there and I felt the air force would be a good thing to get into. So I volunteered. Actually, I'd volunteered before I was called up for the thirty days but I hadn't had an interview at that time. When I come back I was called in for an interview in Moncton. They told me it would be awhile, that they weren't ready yet. Things were just shaping up for training and they would call me later. So, later in the month, I was called up and they asked me what I wanted to be. I said, "Well, I think I'd like to be trained for a pilot."

The fella says, "Now just hold on a minute there. That's the toughest course that we have. For pilot."

I said, "That sounds alright. I don't mind that."

I had been working, loading lumber boats in West Bay, pulp boats in Moose River. As far as the lumber boats, we were on the beach there at six o'clock in the morning to get out to the ships. They were anchored off in West Bay, just off of Parrsboro. We worked ten hours a day. I was used to long days and I didn't figure the air force could throw anything at me any worse than that.

So I said, "It doesn't bother me any if it's a tough course. Sounds interesting."

I took to it! I liked it!

The first enemy planes that I ran into was in England. I had the choice of either going on to fighter planes or being trained more on bomber planes. I thought I'd like to try the fighter planes. So I got onto a 610 squadron. My instructor had been all through the Battle of Britain. He was an excellent gentleman. We were doing coastal patrol. We would fly out and meet ships coming in from Canada and the United States, to chase enemy bombers off. The German air force liked to attack the ships even near the coast. I'll tell you, they were some scared of the Spitfires! If they saw them, boy, they beat it. It was hard to get a crack at them. They'd pop into a cloud in some hurry. It was sort of a cat and mouse game. That was my first contact.

Later on, I was shipped out to Egypt. They were shaping up for the Battle of El Alamein. That was my first contact with actual dogfighting. When you dogfight with an opponent it isn't very long before you think, "I wonder how good he is?" 'Cause some of those fellas, see, they were bragged up to being awful good. All of a sudden you realize he's making mistakes and it sort of makes you think, "Heck! This isn't so bad after all."

We were shaping up to the Battle of El Alamein. Our British forces had been shoved back by Rommel's forces. It was a do or die situation. So they sent out Montgomery to take over.

Now the army and the air force weren't getting along too good. The army was always blaming the air force for not being there when they needed them, when they were being bombed or something. So the air force sent one of our officers to the army as a liaison officer, and the army sent an officer to the air force as liaison. We had a lot better communications back and forth.

Montgomery said it'd be three months before he would even attempt to beat Rommel. It would take three months to get the troops in that he wanted. They had to come all the way around Africa and up the Red Sea and through the Suez Canal. I suppose it was only about two weeks or so before they told us about when the battle would start.

One thing the army requested. They said there's four front-line, enemy aerodromes that, when we start the battle, they're gonna harass our troops. We can't have that if we want to win. The air force has got to destroy those aerodromes!

So our commanding officer says, "That's the order. The army says they'll give us a week to do it. We'll start tomorrow morning, bright and early."

Tomorrow morning it was pouring rain. It was just streaming! And it streamed for four days. It never let up day or night.

After the four days were up, next morning, it cleared off. The sun come out hotter than everything. At noon, as we come out of the mess tent, the commanding officer said, "I just got word a reconnaissance plane took off from Cairo, where there's a cement runway. They took a look at the four front-line aerodromes. They're still bogged in and it's drizzling rain there a little. If it dries up enough by tomorrow, we'll try to take off here."

I had noticed that a slit trench I had dug outside my tent had no water in it. With all that rain, there was no water in it. It was all gravel. It's going right through. So I said to the commanding officer, "Why don't we try to get off today? This afternoon?"

He said, "We can't. We're just walking around in mud. We couldn't get off at all."

I said, "Has anyone ever checked the runway?"

"Well no," he said. "No good to check the runway."

I said, "Sir, you mind if I go check it?"

Well, of course, there was sort of a grin from mostly RAF pilots. I was attached to the RAF and they often referred to me as a colonial pilot and they all had a big grin on their face, you know. So I struck off and there was another Canadian there, a fella from Wolfville. He said, "Clayton, do you mind if I go with you?" I said no and we walked out.

Well, I'll tell you, with all that heat all of a sudden and all that moisture, it's a sweaty thing walking a quarter of a mile or so out to the runway. There was nothing wrong with it at all. You could hardly shove your heel in it. There was a little guck, maybe half an inch on top, where the sand had blown in. See, they had dozed it off and they were down to gravel. The water ran right through it!

We told the commanding officer this and we volunteered to try to take off. "My soul," he said, "those aircraft are so powerful. You open your throttle up, you'll stand her right on the nose! We can't afford to wreck the aircraft."

I said, "No, we won't do that at all. If we can't get off half way down the runway, we'll abort the takeoff."

He said, "You can't get out on it. You can't get out of the parking lot."

I said, "If we get stuck, we shove 'em! All you fellas standing around, get behind the wings and give us a shove!"

So he said, "Alright. You can try it."

Well, we had no trouble at all. My soul, only a quarter of the way down the runway and we were off in the air. And I'm telling you, that commanding officer must have jumped in the nearest plane. He was right on the radio and he says, "Boys, circle and we'll join you!"

As it turned out, we had four squadrons on that aerodrome and they all got off. That afternoon, we cleaned out the four front-line enemy aerodromes and never lost one plane! They were really bogged in. We shot up everything. Every truck, every aircraft. I think even a wheelbarrow, if we saw it.

I like to tell my grandchildren stories. They always liked cats and I always thought this was a cute one. When we were in Egypt, one of the pilots brought home this little kitten that he'd found wandering around, following him, in Cairo. He asked the CO if we could keep it for a mascot. The CO said, "Yes, I don't mind. We used to have a cat but I don't know what happened to it. But you'd better ask the cook because he'll have to feed it."

He went in and asked the cook. The cook said, "Yes. I don't mind having a cat around."

So we kept the little kitten. I think it was a lot older than it looked because it grew so fast and filled out so fast with the cook's feeding it.

He had an odd personality, this cat. He wanted to spread his personality around with everybody. We just had one big mess tent. It didn't matter who you were or your rank, we all ate there. We might be setting around there in the evening, maybe writing a letter or playing cards. The cat would jump up off the floor onto somebody's shoulder. He'd go around your neck to the other shoulder and he'd go, "Purrr." Then he'd hop to the next one. He'd go through the whole group. He never missed one.

We would go out on an early morning raid. It would be dark. We could hardly see the runway. When we come back, we had to be debriefed. Then we'd go from the dispersal tent to have breakfast, usually walking single file because it was sand. Always walking in the same place, so the sand was beat down and you had sort of a path. There'd be about a dozen of us coming out of the dispersal tent. Out would come Stuka! We named him Stuka after the German Stuka dive-bombers. Out he would come, just on the hop! Just coming, as hard as he could run, to meet you. He'd jump off the ground onto one fellow's shoulder. He'd go round the neck, "Purr-r-r," then he'd jump to the next one and he'd go right through the bunch like that. Then he'd get on the ground and away he'd go to the mess tent. He did that every morning. He was welcoming us back!

As the army captured enemy aerodromes, we moved. We were continually on the move, usually about two hundred miles at a jump. We'd fly all our aircraft to that aerodrome and the rest of the crews came in their trucks by road. They'd pack up the mess tents and everything, and we'd move. We were supposed to be completely mobile.

We could never find Stuka when we started to pack up. Nobody knew where he was but he always arrived. He'd stow away on one of the trucks somewhere.

At one particular place, the CO said, "Where's Stuka? I don't see him around."

One of the pilots said, "He came with me. I was just getting in the aircraft, up comes Stuka and he hops right in the cockpit and crawled right down on the floor. He decided he was gonna fly this time! He wasn't going by truck. When I landed, he hopped out and took off like a scared rabbit. So I don't know where he is, but he's around."

The CO said, "You know, I was on the retreat when we were coming the other way. At this particular aerodrome, we had a cat. The stupid thing would crawl up in between the tent (there's two layers of canvas there and there's a little place in the top that gives you some ventilation), and he'd stick his head out there. Late at night he'd let the greatest screech out of him! It'd make your hair stand on end. I've been out myself and banked that with sand. If Stuka tries that stupid trick he can't get up there. That's why I asked where he was."

We were just sitting there for awhile. It was our first night and we wanted to know if the cook, maybe, could get us a cup of coffee. He said he guessed he could. Thought there'd be water enough for that. Water was rationed in the desert.

We were drinking coffee before we packed it in when, all of a sudden, a devilish screech come out from the tent and there was Stuka, with his head stuck out the top of the tent. He let the deadliest howl out of him. It made all of us jump, like there was a big air raid on or something.

That stupid cat did that every night. We were just there a week, luckily, and that cat never did that again after we moved or before.

I really don't know what became of Stuka in the end. I often meant to ask some of them. I got shot down in 1943 and was in hospital. I never rejoined the squadron. I was on aircraft delivery after that. I couldn't pass the physical to get back on the squadron. I was a convoy leader, delivering new aircraft to the squadrons. I had visited the squadron on different times but Stuka wasn't there. I never did find out what happened to him.

Another, that I always thought was kind of cute, is a bear story about Salmon River. I would be about sixteen years old when I took a job in the woods down at Salmon River, about thirty miles from here. It was right in the woods. I was working in the mill.

Anyway, the year before, or that summer, somebody had found a little baby bear in a log. The mother had died somehow. They brought it to the camp and brought it up.

Next winter, they put it in a barrel or a log or something, to sleep in all winter. The next spring, the bear was out and it was back at the camp. It was a year or a year-and-a-half old, and he was getting pretty rambunctious and sort of a nuisance around the camp. So they took and they chained him up.

After the first winter, we moved the mill down where there used to be a farm. Really nice. A big field and all the lumber piled around. There was a barn there.

The fella that run the mill, his wife was cooking and they had a cow to milk for the camp and they had a couple of small children. I used to milk the cow. They just let the cow go to feed all around the field.

Well, they had the bear tied up back of the barn on a rope. Of course, the bear didn't like being tied up. He liked to roam. This day, about three o'clock in the afternoon, the mill was shut down for some reason. The cook said to me, "We haven't got any milk for supper. Would you mind getting the cow in and milking her? Milk it early tonight?"

So a couple of the other young fellas who were working there, they said they'd go with me. They run ahead. I was standing near the barn and the fellas started chasing the cow. Making it run, which I wouldn't have done. It had a little bell on. It wasn't very loud, but as the cow run it made the old bell go quite loud and the bear got all nervoused up. He was jumping around and pulled the collar right off his neck. With the cow running and the boys chasing, why, the bear joins in the frolic. The bear's chasing the cow.

Around and around they go and the cow heads for the barn. I noticed that the barn door is swung half-to, so I jumped out and opened the barn door. I jumped back and said, "Now the cow'll go in the barn and, as they come by me, I'll jump at the bear and scare it off. Get the cow and scare the bear off!"

Well, the bear's just a coming pell-mell for the barn. Straight for the barn. And the old cow, instead of going in the barn, she jumps off sideways. The bear can't stop! So the bear goes into a somersault, it goes over and over, right in the barn door! I could hear the bear hit the wall on the other side of the barn. Kerthump! So I rush up and shut the barn door. I had the bear anyway.

The cow puts its tail up over its back and it takes off into the woods and disappears! We don't know where the cow goes.

The two boys come up and we think it's a great joke. We got the bear instead of the cow. We're standing there laughing like everything. Out comes the cook with the milk pail. She says, "What are you boys laughing at?"

"Nothing," I said.

"Nothing?" she says. "Must be something. Did you get the cow in the barn?"

I said, "Sort of."

"What do you mean, sort of?"

I said, "Well, sort of."

So she walks up to the barn door, opens it, and there was the bear, standing on his hind legs. There she is, eyeball to eyeball with the bear! She looks at it for a second and then slams the door and fastens it. She turned around, the milk pail still in her hand. She throws it down, looks at us and says, "Stupid doggone boys. You can't even tell the difference between a bear and a cow!"

There's a short story but it was sort of comical. I call it the lost platoon. The lost platoon in Halifax.

After we got our wings, we were all sent to Halifax to be shipped overseas. We were at a depot, waiting for the ship to take us to England. One of the pilots got a commission; he was now a pilot officer. So the CO said to him, "Why don't you line up the rest of those fellas there and make a platoon out of them? Take them for a route march around Halifax. Give them something to do! They're just sitting around here."

Fine. He marches us all downtown. Must have been fifty of us anyway. He's behind the group. He puts us in two's and we're marching. He marched us around there for about an hour. It was a nice hot, fine day and we weren't feeling too much like marching. You know. Anyway, we were coming out of a side street and then we turned on to a main street.

In those days Halifax had trolley cars with the wires up. Electric cars that run on overhead power lines. The officer's behind this group of fellas and he orders a left turn. He can see we're coming out into an intersection so he hollers, "Left turn!"

The ones ahead, they left turned and here's two trolley cars, empty, just pulling up to the curb. Well, the officer in charge, he can't see that because he hasn't come around the turn yet. The doors open and we march right into the trolley car. We fill that and it pulls out. The next one pulls up. We're filling it as he comes around the turn and he's hollering, "Halt! Halt! Halt!"

Of course, nobody wants to hear him so they just fill the second one and away it goes. He's left with about six of his platoon. The rest of us all got on the trolley cars.

Well, he's scratching his head for awhile and he says to the other six fellas, "Dismissed! There's not much good of me keeping you here."

He's quite a smart fella because he goes back to the unit, back to the base, and he says to the commanding officer," I marched those fellas around for an hour or an hour and a half. I thought it was such a hot day so I just dismissed them."

"Very good," he said. "Very good."

He didn't dare mention he lost his whole platoon on his first assignment.

It was mostly between Port Greville and Advocate Harbour that I became aware of one of the local driving habits. See, that stretch of road is pretty rough in spots. It's also a very windy and hilly road. The locals, when they come to a rough bit, simply veer over and drive on the wrong side. Makes perfect sense. I even tried it myself a few times. Advocate Harbour, by the way, is where we've just arrived.

Paul Spicer

You want to go way back to 1765? Robert come here with his wife and children and a slave.

He eloped. He was a lieutenant in the British navy and he eloped with either Priscilla Cromwell or Priscilla Chalmly. They come up Five Islands way and then they walked down and built a house on Spencer's Island. Then he left that farm to some of the sons and moved to Advocate and started another farm.

The Acadians had been here before that. This was how the place got its name. Advocate.

Just about three weeks ago I was into Spicer's Cove. I was video taping and when I swung the camera around to take a picture going up to Spicer's Cove, all of a sudden it hit me — my father walked this same beach, and his father, and his grandfather. And me and my children have all walked that same beach.

I wrote a poem right there in about twenty minutes, because if I didn't I'd lose the idea.

Spicer's Cove

At Spicer's Cove one sunny day, as I let my thoughts go free,
I thought of past generations and these came flooding to me.
My dad walked over this beach, as his own father did before
And his grandfather also walked it, enjoying it I am sure.

I have walked this beach for years
    and my children along with me.
Camped and picnicked on it, enjoying the rugged beauty.
The gentle surf on the beach or fierce waves in a storm,
As it has been since creation, before any of us were born.

The herring that was caught here, the small boats they did build.
The families they did raise and memories of the old water-mill.
Gathering driftwood from the beach
    from Squally Point to Halibut Head.
Salting meat and storing garden
    for the long winter months ahead.

My dad told me the stories and I have passed them on
To any who will listen, of the times that are gone.
I hope that I may live to see my grandchildren after me
Run, play and gather dulse as Spicers have for centuries.

The poetry I wrote as a kid, I just thought it was stupid, you know. I just thought that nobody would ever enjoy it and that it was just stupid. So I destroyed it 'til I was about thirty years old.

I was in the hospital with Mac Spicer from Spencer's Island. We were in there about seven days. He was saying he was doing a history on the Spicers. So I told him that I was writing poems. He said, "Oh, I'd love to read them."

My wife brought them down and he encouraged me. He read 'em and liked them. He encouraged me, so I started putting some in a little paper. Scott Paper, that was the company I drove for then, had a little monthly paper, *The Wooden Wheel News*. I started putting them in that. And that's when I first started having them printed or published.

The supervisor of the woodland was Bob Murray, at the time, and sometimes we had to wait to get unloaded. There'd be a big line-up of trucks, or something would break down and you couldn't get unloaded. So I wrote this one in about twenty minutes one day. I wrote it on a cardboard off a fanbelt. It started out

Mister Robert Murray, Supervisor of the Woodland Division,
Abercrombi Point, Care of Scott Maritimes Limited.

Dear Mister Murray,
Perhaps you won't mind if I should call you Bob.
I'm writing this letter to you, concerning my truck driving job.
I don't mind the job so much,
    though the hours are early and late.
The worst part of it is to sit in the yard and wait.

I'm not blaming anyone but I would like to know,
When it comes to unloading trucks, why it is so slow.
I thought perhaps you could answer this
    or get things on the ball
And put my troubled mind at ease.
Yours very truly, Paul.

I have another one here. I read in school sometimes, grades one to five, and they enjoy it.

We have a son in Petawawa, Ontario, but he was in Bosnia. He had a young son, maybe a year old or a little less. You could call in a radio station and they would broadcast messages to the guys over there. So I wrote this one for the family but I call it "The Grandson." His name is Dillon.

Just a short note Dillon for you to share with Mum
And for you to help cheer her, as man of the house, Grandson.
For there will be, sometimes while Daddy is gone,
That Mum will need your smile to help her get along.

All the new things you learn and each new tooth you receive.
Also each new word you learn, Mum will be happy
    with each of these.
Grampy is older and wiser now so that is how
    he knows these things.
For he remembers, back years ago,
    the joys that they would bring.

Now I want to share with you a secret for us, Grandson.
Oh, you may share it in the family.
You have the world's greatest Mum.
This will make Dad happy, when you share it with him too.
Also share with them the love I'm sending along to you.

194

For Dad will sure miss you while he is so far away
Doing peace-keeping duties so there may come a day,
That in that land of Bosnia, hostilities may soon cease
And that the people there will once again know peace.

I will close this note now for I must write my son too.
He will want to hear from home. God bless. I love each of you.

Love, Grampy

Here's the one I called "Grandad's Pea Pod Boat."

He went into the garden to get a filled-out pea.
Selected one that suited and this he showed to me.
He took a knife from his pocket and carefully cut along the line.
Then skillfully removed the peas. One, two, six, eight or nine.

The peas he shared with me as I watched, not asking why.
I knew he had something to show me,
    from his smile and twinkling eye.
With a twig to hold the sides apart,
    he put it in some water to float.
I remember well, him showing me,
    how to make the pea pod boat.

He said it could be a ship of dreams that I could sail
    the whole world wide.
Visiting ports both near and far
    and see strange, new countrysides.
I visited so many countries in that world of "let's pretend"
And in that ship from a pea pod,
    I sailed the world and back again.

Gone now is the world of "let's pretend"
    for reality has filled it in.
But make a child a pea pod boat and it lives all over again.

I printed two books myself but I'm a poor business man. I'd give 'em away quicker than I'd sell 'em. I may do it again. People have really encouraged me, you know, and a lot of people enjoy them. Usually they're printed in *The Citizen*, a local paper. I know some people that have some of them on their fridges for encouragement.

This was the very first car and I was pretty proud of it.

My first car, when I was seventeen
And I was as happy as anyone could have been.
I know that many thought it a wreck
But I was proud of that '49 Chevrolet.

I patched up the trunk and I patched up the floor
And for parking in winter caulked the passenger door.
I lied about my age, a license to get
But I sure had fun in that old Chevrolet.

Five dollars worth of gas would go a long way
And I guess that it should, for it was a day's pay.
The good times we had I'll never forget
Or the places we went in that old Chevrolet.

The police often stopped me and I never tried to run
For I wasn't doing wrong, just out having fun.
They found nothing wrong, though many times they did check
The mechanical condition of that old Chevrolet.

After two years, the old car gave out
From neglect and abuse. Here I've no doubt.
I've had many cars since but you can bet
I'll always remember that old Chevrolet.

This one's about a '47 Dodge but it was in great shape. An old feller had it. He took great care of it but he finally got old and he hit a bridge railing and tore a fender off. So then his family didn't want him to drive it any more and a bootlegger got it. He used to go to Moncton to bring liquor down. The Mounties had been watching it. After I bought it, whenever they saw the car on the road, they stopped it. So this was it.

The '47 Dodge

I bought it from a bootlegger who was known as Freddy Fox.
I didn't know at the time the car was being watched
But before I had gone two miles, I was going to quickly learn,
For the police stopped me
        and searched the car from stem to stern.

They told me to keep it off the road
     until I got it transferred in my name
Or that I would be fined if they stopped me once again.
I quickly got it transferred and am alright now, I'm thinking
But the very next time I headed out,
     in the rear-view a red light is blinking.

They searched that car thoroughly,
     in hiding places I didn't know existed.
Asked questions until I was so confused,
     that I got my own name twisted.
I kept that car nearly a year and never had to pay no fines
But I'm sure they checked it at least thirty-five times.

I don't think they ever believed that I was just out having fun.
Yet you would think that they would learn
     that I wasn't running rum.
I suppose I should be thankful, for it always kept me straight
But it sure was embarrassing to go out on a date.

Especially after a couple of times, in either sunshine or rain,
As we had to get out of the car
     while they searched it once again.
The girls got suspicious too and, though I tried to explain
That I wasn't a wanted man,
     they weren't quick to go with me again.

Finally I sold the car and was overjoyed, to say the least
When I could go out for a drive
     and not be stopped by the police.

It was kind of embarrassing to be stopped though, all the time.

Our church pastor, in '95, said there weren't many Mother's Day songs and he said, "How about writing one?"

So I said, "Sure." Kind of on the spur of the moment. And I did. The minister's son's a pianist and he put music to it and the men's choir sung it in church. It went over good. I can't sing it but I'll read it.

There's an old rocking chair, near the window,
 that often brings sweet memories.
Though it is still now and silent,
 it tells of a mother's love for me.
That old chair, in my childhood, was a refuge from all daily care.
When the hurts of the world overwhelmed,
 Mother would comfort me there.

Its gentle squeaks were so soothing,
 much like the touch of Mother's hand.
It was here I could pour out my sorrows
 and Mother would always understand.
From this chair she taught many lessons
 and healed many hurts, I am sure.
Here too, she thanked God in heaven,
 for his love and mercies, once more.

Some lessons I learned there from Mother
 have these many years been a guide.
They show of kindness and wisdom,
 when with love, they are applied.
I regret now sorrows I caused her
 for I know many times I caused her pain.
Yet I know that for me, though unworthy,
 she would gladly do it all again.

Apple River was always called The Bar. There was a sandbar there. This was where we used to go out and coast down the hill. You had no TV or radio and it was cold in the winter time. I remember water freezing on the stove at nights, it'd be so cold. And you'd hear the trees just snapping, the nights would be so cold. And the walks to school. There was no school buses and very few cars. There was some hard times at that time.

Us young fellas, we hunted when we was just eleven or twelve — hunted partridge and rabbit because sometimes that was all we had to eat. It was just hard times and we learned to hunt for food. But we'd always been warned not to kill anything that we weren't gonna eat. Anything that we killed would be ate. And we got good enough, my brother and I both, to light matches with a .22.

My brother was a marksman all the time he was in the army. I don't know if I could shoot now or not but I think I could. But I haven't shot for years. I've no need to. People ask me why I don't hunt and I just said, "Well, I'm not hungry."

This was a country school we went to at The Bar. In school, we were allowed to wear slingshots around our neck and the crotch hanging down the back, as long as they stayed on your neck.

Down at West Apple River where I learned my ABC's
The schoolhouse has long been gone,
 the fields grown up in trees.
It wasn't anything fancy, like some schools today.
It was just a simple room but served the purpose anyway.

It was a plain country school, of bygone days it seems.
With barefooted children in summer
 and patched-up old blue jeans.
When the weather permitted and we promised
 to run away no more
We'd move our desks outside and have our lessons outdoors.

We spent many happy hours in summer,
 studying Mother Nature's ways.
Finding birds' nests or fossils,
 it seemed better than books anyway.
Some children were marksmen with slingshots,
 some others at climbing trees.
Some were expert at annoying the teacher
 and still others in a spelling bee.

If we cut our hands or feet, the remedy at the time
Was wrap it in a clean white cloth and pour on the turpentine.
In winter we often had to shift further from
 or nearer the stove.
The ones who sat too close were hot,
 while the ones further away froze.

There's many a story of a red school,
 that some may recall with delight,
But our country school was always painted white.
I can still see the sign, in my mind it will always stick.
West Apple River School, Section Number 26.

I was always good at reading. We had spelling bees and I loved them because I was a good speller when I was a young fella. I never got a strapping all the time I went to school. No. I was too frightened of the teachers, I guess. I was usually pretty good.

A lot of children have liked this story; it's a real life story. When I was trucking, we had a dog then named Woody. And the youngest feller was three years old. He looked out the window, this was about a week before Easter, and the dog had a rabbit out there. So this was the story.

> We have four children, eight, seven, five and three.
> They have a little dog that they call Woody.
> I got home from work one night and found
>   the youngest lad in tears.
> Crying like his heart had been broke for his whole three years.
>
> I asked him, "What's the trouble, to make a little boy so sad?"
> And through his tears he told me that, "Woody dog is bad."
> The story that he told me, it later struck me funny.
> The words he said were, "Daddy, Woody ate the Easter Bunny."
>
> The dog had come home with a rabbit that it got somewhere.
> Perhaps caught it in the woods or took it from a snare.
> I comforted him for a while and told him not to fear.
> That when the time came, the Easter Bunny would be here.
>
> Every time I think about it, I can hear the little fellow sob.
> And if he lives forever, I don't believe he'll forgive that dog.

He was home just the other day and I was talking about it. He said, "I think I've forgiven the dog." Yeah. Yeah.

I like to tell this story. My wife and I played together when we was children. Her grandparents lived in Apple River. West Apple River actually. When they'd come in to visit, I'd go down and play with her. So . . .

> When just small children, a dream had we
> As we played together under the lilac tree.
> Or set for hours on the old lawn swing
> Or skipped for a drink, down to the spring.

We watched the squirrels run along the pole fence
Sometimes gathering food as they went.
And who was more merry, them or we,
As we played and dreamed under the lilac tree?

We were so young, just six and nine then
As we dreamed together, a lifetime we'd spend.
Now forty years later, by God's good grace,
We recall when we played at your grandparents' place.

For fourteen years later, our dreams were realized
And on a fine summer day, you became my bride.
Now sometimes, while talking, we tell our family
Of the plans we made under the lilac tree.

So I haven't really gone very far away from where I was born and brought up. I was away for a few years in New Brunswick. The poem about the '47 Dodge, that's where I was. But I was only drifting for about four years, then I come back. Been here ever since. I love the place. It's a beautiful place. It's beautiful country.

When I was just a young fella, maybe seven or eight years old, we lived right close to what we call The Bar. And the twelfth of July was a big Orangemen's day there, where people took their picnic lunches. There'd be three or four hundred people there, which was a lot of people. And one of the fads for young fellers at that time was pop covers. These was old pop bottle caps. You took the cork outta them and you put the cork on the inside of your shirt and then put the pop cover on over it. An' it would stick to your shirt. Well, whoever had the most pop covers on their shirt was the hero kind of thing.

So I was down one Sunday morning, probably ten o'clock, to get pop covers before anyone else. But I was just filling my pockets. I'd take 'em home and put 'em on my shirt. All of a sudden there was nothing! No sound! Nothing! It was just like a vacuum. A stillness that would make you look around to see what was wrong. Which is what I did of course. I looked up. I saw an animal running towards the water on its hind legs. It had long hind legs and shorter front ones. It had a body like a kangaroo maybe but kind of a horse's head. Not as big. Well, I didn't stick around to see what it was gonna do or where it went. I went the other way. Probably faster that it went towards the water.

I told the story a few times and, of course, people just said you're lying. Or you're making it up. Or you was imagining things. You got so at last that you didn't tell it.

But one time I was telling some relatives of my wife's. When I started describing this animal, this guy looked kinda funny at me and I thought to myself, "Yeah, I shouldn't have told it."

When I finished, he said, "You know, one time my father was sick and he described that animal, exactly like you're describing it, at the foot of his bed."

And probably eight or ten years ago now, in Pictou, it was on the radio. It was down around Pictou that different people had saw this here animal and they described the same thing as what I saw.

I'm sure we didn't all imagine the same thing.

Anyway, I never saw anything more there and I fished lobster there for years. I was there all hours of the day and night.

Before we were married, my wife and I, we was in there one evening. We had a '63 Volkswagen, which was our wedding car, and we was parked out there. I hadda go to the bathroom so I got outta the car, you know, and there was some trees there. When I come back we was sitting there talking, making wedding plans, and it sounded like a limb scratching across the roof of the car. So I was quite brave and, of course, showing off. Well, I didn't think anything about it because I thought that's what it was. I got outta the car anyway to look, to see what was doing it. There was nothing anywhere near the car and there was no place anybody could hide near it, to play a trick on me. So I got back in the car and a few minutes later it sounded like somebody took a chain, put it around the bumper, and started dragging it around the bumper. I didn't get out that time to see if there was anything touching my car, now I'll tell you! We got right outta that! And I've heard other people tell the same about going there parking.

There was another place just down the road from it, we'd hear voices every time we went there. The house was gone but there was a shed. So I said to my wife, "Well, you watch."

So I got out and walked around the shed. I said, "Did you see anyone?" She said, "No." So I went inside the shed. There was nothing in there except a big old lobster crate. There was nothing in that and no place for anybody to hide.

But those were the only two places, of all the places that I've parked or went, that anything unusual ever happened. Some people would call it a lotta things. And other people have had the same experiences on The Bar.

There was a guy that lived in Salem here, Ben Jarrett. They used to say he was possessed with the devil. Others said that he was devilish. That he wasn't possessed with the devil, that he was just devilish. But there were some great stories told about him.

Some nights he would leave Salem, New Salem, and he would go through the woods to Eatonville, in the middle of the night. It wouldn't matter to him. And other times he'd be so scared he wouldn't go outside alone.

One time he'd gone back there to get the mill ready for Monday morning. Get the boiler fired up. He made a fire and this was one of his times that he wasn't scared. Apparently he started a fire up and he thought he heard something. So he opened the boiler door to see if there was anything in there. Well, somebody had been drinking some and they'd gone in there and crawled in this dutch oven. It was still quite warm in there, you know. He took a poker and reached in and pulled him out. I guess it didn't hurt him none.

They used to tell a story about one feller that nobody ever saw working. Yet he always had a tree cut when the teamster would go back. They claimed that if anybody touched his axe, he would break the handle out of it and put a new one in. He wouldn't see this but, someway, he would know if the axe was touched.

This same fella, they told the story about . . . one night the lumber crew got in bed. 'Course, you had lower bunks and upper bunks. Quite often the people in the upper bunks was warm and the ones in the lower bunks'd be cold.

Some of the crew had made a fire an he got up and opened the door. Somebody else got up and closed it. And he got up and opened it again. Somebody got up and closed it and took an axe and they drove it in the door jamb so that it couldn't open. They just got back in bed and the axe flew across the room and the door come open.

These was a few of the ones that I remembered.

We leave the Parrsboro shore and drive to Springhill where I get to sit on the Liar's Bench and swap yarns with a few old miners. Our destination though is the home of one-time miner.

Harry Munroe

A Coalminer's Life

My dad was a coalminer and my granddad too.
They worked their whole lives down in old Number 2.
Their lives they spent working, from daylight 'til dark
So their families they could feed and give them a start.

A coalminer's life was hard at its best
As deep underground, the work gave no rest.
The dust they would breathe deep into their lungs,
So old men they were while they were yet young.

They worked in dangers, explosions and bumps
To mine the coal, our economy to pump.
For coal reigned as king during that era of time
And many a young man would enter the mine.

I started working underground at sixteen years of age
As being a coalminer was then the rage.
To do my best, I was determined to try.
Although many friends you would see die.

And also there was the storyteller so fine.
So, on the liar's bench, they would pass the time.
As each one, by story, they would try to outdo
The things that had happened in old Number 2.

So of this, my friends, you can be sure,
These brave men of the deep were really mature.
They were buddies to me at an important time.
So I'll always remember them as friends of mine.

Like the poem says, coalmining was the work to do at that time. From listening to both my father and grandfather talking about the mines and so on, I think I was pretty well aware of what it would be like. Because these men talked quite often about what it was like down in the mines, the working conditions, and some of the problems they had to overcome in work.

I started on what was called the ten-two wall. That meant I was down 10,200 feet. And because I was a tall, slim fella and number two seam was about ten feet high, I was given the job of second man on the packs, building packs to hold up the roof. As the coal miners would dig the coal, they would prepare for a pack as they advanced into the coal. The second man on the packs lifted the pack sticks off the pans, the shaker pans, as the wood would come down.

Then you had the builder. He would be inside the mine and it was built like a log cabin. Two sticks one way, two another and you just kept building up that way. It was six by eight by six feet, the pack sticks were, and that was hardwood so it was quite a heavy task.

First they were gonna give me boy's pay because you had to be eighteen to get man's pay. But when I went to the manager, Mr. Campbell, and told him what I was doing he said, "Well, that's a man's job. You'll get man's pay." Which I did.

Man's pay then was $3.74 a day and boy's pay was just $3. So seventy-four cents a day seemed to be a lot of money.

The only time I ever really had fear, that I would call fear, was at the time of the explosion in Number 4. In 1956, I was in the second draeger crew and they sent us over. [Draegermen were coal miners trained for underground rescue work. They were named for Alexander Draeger, a German scientist, who developed special oxygen equipment used in gas-filled mines.] They'd sent a crew down the main slope from the bankhead. They were only down about two hundred feet or less and two of the draegermen were down. They'd been overcome by gas. I realized I was like the new kid on the block. I was a novice, as far as draeger training. I'd only been a draegerman about two years and this was our first real test. We used to go once a month and have draeger training, but it's a little different when you're facing the real thing. Then you look down and you see these experienced men that were down and you begin to think, "What chance have I got?"

There was a lot of confusion. Some were saying, "Don't touch this. Don't touch that. Don't do this. Don't do that." So it was just like mass confusion.

So yes, I had some trepidation I'll tell you when I went down. But once I went down there and we brought up the first man, Alex Spence, that gave me complete confidence in the draeger breathing apparatus. After that, I had no fear of the machine. But it was that very first, initial impact, when you looked down and you see what you'd refer to as the experienced or old-timers that have got into difficulty. We lost two draegermen right there on that slope.

When you left home to go to work, you left in what they refer to as your street clothes. And you would go to the washhouse, or the changehouse, and get into your pit clothes. The washhouse is like a big barn, and rather than having lockers they had buckets. They had a pulley way up in the peak of the roof, if you get the idea, with a rope and a bucket with hooks on it. You'd drop your bucket down. You'd put your street clothes in it — your shoes in the bucket and you'd hang your clothes on the hooks. Then you haul her up. So it wouldn't take much space. That was the way it was. So then, you got into your pit clothes and then you'd go to the lamp cabin. And of course, that's where I had this poem.

The Lamp Cabin Story

To help the miners down deep in the mine
They must have a lamp that will really shine.
To light up the roadway and the long wall
And to help them timber the roof, so it won't fall.

So from the washhouse to the lamp cabin they must go
And to pick up their lamp, a check number they must show
To indicate they were entering the deep.
And the boys in the lamp cabin, their tally they would keep.

Now the lamp cabin boys were humorously inclined
And sometimes tell a story, if you had the time.
There was Ralph, Harry and Jim.
They were men that the miner's had confidence in.

And when the miners came up out of the mine
For the lamp cabin they would make a beeline.
To turn in their lamp and pick up their check
From one of the boys that they had come to respect.

So the lamp cabin was just another part
Of a miner's life from the very start.
And though those boys never entered the mine
They provided the needed light with a lamp that would shine.

When you come up out of the mines, you reverse the situation. You turn your lamp in and you pick up your check number. And then you head to the washhouse to go back into your street clothes. The washhouse has the showers and so on. So I have a poem about "The Coal Miner's Washhouse Blues." It's interesting what would happen there. This is how the poem goes.

You come out of the mines covered with grime and dirt
And you head for the washhouse to take off your shirt.
You go to the showers so grave and bold
And turn on the water only to find that it's cold.

And the air outside, it's chilly and cold
So to take a shower one must be bold.
But shower you must in order to be clean
But the boilers can't supply all of the steam.

Sometimes the water, it might be hot
But most of the time it's really not.
So under the showers with the greatest of ease
And hold your breath as you try not to freeze.

So the washhouse blues you can never forget
And how your buddies would frown and fret.
But of one thing you can be sure
When you'd come out of the shower,
      somebody would open the door.

So a cold blast of air you were sure to get.
That's why the washhouse blues we'll never forget.
But after all, it was a way of life
So we'll always remember it the rest of our life.

I mentioned stories and so forth. I can always remember one of the old storytellers that used to sit on the liar's bench. His name was Perce Tabor. Us young fellas, we'd gather around him because he had a way of telling a story.

One I always remember he told. On a Friday, he told us young fellas that he was gonna go fishing on the weekend. So we thought to ourselves, "Well, we're gonna get a real good story about this."

So on Monday, back to work. We waited and waited for the story from him. Nothing was forthcoming. Finally, during lunch, we approached Perce to find out, how did the fishing go? We expected this normal story about the big one that got away. You know?

"Well," he said, "I've decided to give up fishing."

Of course, we said, "Well what happened? Big one get away?"

And he said, "Oh no. No, no. The fish I caught was so small, I had to take 'em to the jewellers and get them cleaned!"

I can remember that one very well.

I wrote a poem about story time in the pesthouse. Before the miners went into the mine, under the bankhead there's a place they called the pesthouse. You went in and you filled your water can. They had some benches in there for when the weather was inclement. In the winter it was heated. I tell you, there was some pretty good storytellers in there too. I don't know where the word pesthouse come from. I guess that it was just one of the local sayings. So they would just go in there and sit and wait and tell the stories and so on. That's all I know about it. We always referred to it as the pesthouse.

Storytime in the Pesthouse

Under the bankhead, in the Pesthouse of Number 2,
There's a story going around that just can't be true.
So some would listen intently while others would talk.
But to some of the stories you can't take much stock.

There's some would tell of their aches and pains
While others would tell of their stress and strains.
They would all seem to promote some miracle cure
That they had bought at the local drugstore.

Sometimes their stories were in serial form,
Just like the soap operas that are the norm.
Some would just sit and chew and spit
While others would demonstrate their humour and wit.

My father would leave home shortly after lunch
To hear the full story from that story-telling bunch.
And each one would add a line or two
Until they really believed that the stories were true.

I learned through the years not to doubt these wise men
Because a long life of experience they could transcend.
So the younger ones would quietly show their respect
To the long-winded stories that they could expect.

I guess you'd say the pesthouse was almost like an attraction. And it was a great thing for the company because these storytellers, you know, would actually be a source of encouragement for people to go to work. And sometimes too, perhaps the stories seemed to alleviate a lot of the fear, or whatever, of the mines.

This was by a man by the name of Red Gallagher. You notice a lot of miners had nicknames. Now Red, he had red hair. Played ball and so on. So a lot of them, you never knew their first name because all you ever heard was the nickname.

This Red Gallagher was telling a story one day. They were talking about dogs and how smart dogs were and he was telling about a dog he had. It was a dog for catching raccoons. He said, "In fact, that dog was so smart you could put the stretchboard out on the step, the dog would look at it, and go to the woods and bring back a raccoon."

But he said, one day his mother forgot and put the ironing board out. The dog has never come back! He's still looking yet!

Now these men all claim that these are true stories. True life experiences.

I enjoy country music, and I started writing songs when I was about sixteen. In fact, away back when I was sixteen, I made a demo disc which I gave to, I'm tryin' to think of his name, over in Summerside. They gave it some airtime. That was way back in the '40s. But poems, it's only been the last eight or ten years. Some of these stories, well, I thought I'd put them in poem form at least.

I've written one called "The Town Called Springhill." It starts out

> There's an old mining town of high renown
>   and it sits on top of a hill.
> I remember it well so this story I tell about
>   the town called Springhill.

Then in the next verse I go on to show how

> Coal was found deep underground and digging it
>   took great skill.
> And miners would toil deep down in the soil for the coal
>   that was under the hill.

And then I go into the mine disasters. See, the first disaster was the explosion in Number 4, in '56. Then the bump in '58. So then I say,

> Number 4 blew before Number 2,
>   in two different tragic events.
> An explosion and bump gave the town a great thump
> And brave miners were laid to rest.

Then the next verse is the rescue part. So I guess what I'm trying to capture is the event, either by poem or by song.

Here's another poem. After you leave that pesthouse, to go down the mines you ride on what they call the trolleys. Keeping in mind that the seam of coal is on an incline of about thirty degrees so, when you're talking about down 13,000 feet, or whatever, that's not straight up and down. That's on an incline. So when you go down in the trolleys, it's just a miniature flatcar with straps nailed across and you sit on them. The incline is what keeps you from sliding off. This is about riding on the trolleys.

To enter the mines, by the trolleys you must go.
But to some, they seem to travel so slow.
Especially when they were on their way home.
So some would sit, complain and moan.

And some, when they were entering into the deep,
Would sit in the trolleys and go to sleep.
While others were anxious to reach the incline
So that the coal they could mine.

Now sometimes the trolleys would give a jerk
As men were being lowered down to work.
Some from fear, their chewing they'd swallow,
While others would just sit there and holler.

The top seat in the trolleys was considered the best
Because, while riding, they could lay back and rest.
While in the rest of the seats you were cramped and squeezed
As the ones in front of you would lay back at ease.

So if you ever go into a mine
Don't forget to keep this in mind.
Make for the top seat in the trolleys to ride
Then your trip will be pleasant, with comfort on your side.

You get the idea? As you're sitting there the man in front of you is sitting between your legs. And they just lay right back on you. So you had all their weight. They just totally relaxed. Some were so relaxed they'd go to sleep when they were going down the mines.

The liar's bench in Springhill is in the same location it always was. On that particular road, where the liar's bench is, there was a group of row houses. Miners' row houses. There's only one house left there now. They were double houses. The liar's bench was a place for the miners to gather in the evening or morning, depending on their shift. They'd just sit around and tell stories. Of course, the young people would gather around to listen to them. Like I mention in this poem here. This is just one verse out of it.

And also there was the storyteller's so fine.
So on the liar's bench they would pass the time.
As each one, by story, they would try to outdo
The things that happened in old Number 2.

It was a form of recreation for them. It kept the group close together.

I wrote this poem because it was my first experience in the mines. It says

When just a young lad of sixteen years
From working in the mines I had no fear.
I was assigned to work in the ten-two.
I'm telling you that was quite a crew.

To "Red" Bob Smith I would report.
He was a man who could get out of sorts.
I was assigned second man on the packs
And you had little time to relax.

Now as you would travel up the longwall
Then to each miner you would call
To see if they were ready for you to build a pack
That would hold up the roof over their back.

Now there was Percy Tabor, Ray and Dick.
Of them, Percy would use the pick.
While Ray and Dick would shovel the coal
As down the shaker pans it would roll.

The rest of the miners of that longwall crew
Worked the buddy system that they best knew
Because their safety depended upon each other.
So to each one they became just like a brother.

Once in awhile you'd get a bump.
Sometimes it would really make you jump.
And after the coal dust it would clear
Then you would put behind any fear.

See, after you got a bump, the whole mine would fill with coal dust. And you couldn't see a thing for awhile. But then it would settle down again. After a bump, you got a lot of snapping and cracking as everything was just settling. It was relieving the pressure.

Now, going into the longwall they were all on one tally, about thirty men working on it. They had an expression in there about a longwall fattening stall. Some of the men didn't pull their weight. This poem came about not too long ago. I was talking with a buddy and this is how these ideas come for poems. We got talking about some of the men that didn't carry their weight in the longwall and how they called them the longwall fattening stalls. I come home and I just wrote. Sat down and put the poem together. It goes like this.

> Of the thirty men working on the longwall
> You always had one or two fattening stalls.
> These were men who worked on the coal face
> But with the other men they never kept pace.
>
> The men of the longwall had their tally
> So the number of loaded boxes was their rally.
> As well as the timber that they would install
> To help boost the pay of the men on the longwall.
>
> Sometimes they'd be paid for shovelling out
> Or the hard bench they had to jackhammer out.
> To get the wall ready for a shift of the pans
> Which was carried out by the company hands.
>
> Now it made no difference if the coal was close or far away.
> Those in the fattening stalls never really earned their pay.
> So, as they dallied their time on the longwall,
> Their workplace was referred to as the fattening stall.

So you can see, miners also had a sense of humour. They figure these guys are just there to get fat, so to speak, not to work!

This is a song I wrote last spring and I call this "Brave Men of the Deep."

Deep underground where the sun never shines
You'll find men working in the coal mines.
These are men who have very little fear
Of the dangers that are always lurking so near.

They never talk about what might happen to them.
Some type of disaster, that their life, it might end.
Because coal mining is a way of life
And to this these brave men have given their life.

It's hard to imagine the hardships they endure.
From the sagging roof that they try to secure
Or the dust they breathe deep into their lungs.
So old men they become while they are still young.

When they see a fellow worker injured or killed
It is with sadness that their hearts are filled.
Because they realize that a buddy and friend
Has been lost, when their life it came to an end.

So always remember those brave men of the deep
Some will be working while you are asleep.
So here's to the miners down deep in the mine.
Into a world where the sun never shines.

It's interesting sometimes. I don't go out of my way to write poems but when an idea comes into my mind then it just clicks together and it just rolls out. I've been in the Anne Murray Centre a dozen times at least but one day last summer when we come out the idea clicked about writing a poem. I just entitled it

Our Hometown Girl

There is a girl from our hometown
Who has gained international renown
Because she has a beautiful singing voice
And has made many a heart rejoice.

She started out with Singalong Jubilee
And they aired the show on the CBC.
It was from this humble start
That she has won the people's hearts.

Then there was the Snowbird song.
It was a tune that did catch on.
Brought Anne into international fame
So she became a household name.

She also has her many awards
Which has struck a happy chord.
From Grammys and Junos and all the rest
To the hometown folks she is the best.

So if you visit our friendly town,
You'll see the people as they gather around.
For a visit to the Anne Murray Centre they come
To learn about Anne and the things she has done.

Our storytelling time is almost over, for now. Just one more stop, near Tatamagouche, Nova Scotia to visit Lester Tattrie, just outside of town on French River Road.

Lester Tattrie

Family and friends were coming in for my eighty-fifth birthday and I wrote this a few days before.

> All the years, they did go by, I'm eighty-five today.
> With family and friends around me, I'm feeling very gay.
> I've had my share of hardships and troubles by the score
> But if I count my blessings, I'm sure they'll number more.
>
> My days on earth are numbered, how many I'm not sure.
> But I'm lookin' forward to that day I'll walk that golden shore.
> I'll be with my friends and family and then I hope to see
> Where we'll always be together, throughout eternity.

In my younger days I guess I didn't have time to think or write. I was working all the time.

They bought me a new pair o' boots. Kinda like a coarse boot, you know, a work boot. Anyway, I went to school with them on and I started to take the measles. I didn't know it and I played out coming home. I was jawing about the boots playing my legs out. I sat down on the road and my first cousins over here they were going to school, Dad's brother's children. They coaxed me and finally got me up and I got home. Well, I found out the next morning what was the matter, when I was all broke out in measles. Nothing the matter with the boots.

Some of the family was coaxing me for to write something like this and I did. I was getting up in years then and I suppose, maybe, they wanted something to remember me by.

> In the year of nineteen hundred and eight, when my parents
>   they were young,
> On November the twenty-third, was born to them a son.
> He was his mother's pride and his father's joy.
> Would sell a few pounds of butter just to buy him a toy.
>
> And now that I am seven and to the school did start,
> When I'm in the classroom I'm never very smart.
> I took up my grade eight's work, this I did not pass
> And when I left the schoolroom, I left it very fast.
>
> I got a job in the sawmill, worked ten hours a day.
> I only made a dollar. That's all that they did pay.
> And now I'm almost twenty and to the west did go
> To work in the harvest fields, until it did snow.
>
> Now I'm all through working way out in the west.
> I'm getting back aboard the train, just hoping for the best.
> I land back in Tatamagouche, from where I did depart.
> Seems so nice to be back, puts a flutter in my heart.
>
> I took all of my money and I bought a Model T
> And when I went out driving, was when I felt so free.
> I got myself a girlfriend, I thought her very sweet.
> When we went out driving, we sat so close together, you'd think
>   there was only one in the seat.
>
> And when I did propose to her it was coming on the fall.
> I had to ask her daddy and it took a lot of gall.
> But now, as we are married and a family we did start,
> We got a little baby girl we hold next to our heart.

And every two years after, when I walked through the door,
This is what I'd hear my wife say, "I'm pregnant once more."
We have ten of a family living and eight own their own homes.
But two are still with us 'cause they did not care to roam.

And now I'm past my three score year and ten.
I'll stop this foolish writing and I'll lay away my pen.

I don't know if I should tell this or not but I took her sister home and I met my wife! It's over sixty-seven years.

The Weatherby Family Reunion,
Tatamagouche, Nova Scotia. August the 14th, 1993.

Come all my friends and relatives, when this reunion you attend.
Could I have your attention, to these few lines I pen.
Here's to Fred Weatherby, his frame is tall and thin.
He married Annie Tattrie.
That's where the Weatherby family began.

They had a large family, nine or ten, I'm not sure.
But when I start to count them, I'm sure I will get more.
There was Stanley and there's Ross and there was Cecil too.
There was Lizzy and there's Ethel and Edith and Lily too.

Now don't you get discouraged folks,
        'cause I'm not nearly through.
There was Helen and there's Effie, there's Viola and Mary too.
But I'll not forget Cathy, to her I said, "I do."
There's Weatherbys, there's Tattries and there's Hawkins too.
There's MacKeils and there's Dobsons and there's Colpitts too.

And there's some I cannot name
For the only time I saw them was their picture in a frame.
The branches on this family tree are spread out far and wide.
Some across Canada, some off to the U.S. border,
        on the other side.

The sad part of this story of the Weatherby family,
There's only two still with us on this special day.
The rest is gone to heaven, to that great city far away.
And this family reunion will soon be in the past.
The next great reunion will forever last.

I remember well, Mother used to call it the forerunner. She had a brother lived in Westchester. She was over to her dad's brother's one evening, getting dusk, and her brother had one little fellow, I don't know how old he'd be, maybe five or six. She was coming home and there was a path across the field here. When she come out, and along the line, there's a swale runs up there. She walked over and crossed the culvert. When she was crossing the culvert, this little figure appeared, in white, in the swamp. Scared her pretty bad but she stood there and watched it. It went up the swamp and disappeared.

The next morning, she got word that the little fella was burnt to death. I often heard her tell that story. That's what she called a forerunner.

There was only one time that I ever saw anything. I don't know yet what it was. One winter the snow was awful deep. I was in my teens. Anyway, Dad was working in Millbrook in a sawmill. He'd come home on Saturday nights. Millbrook's about six or seven miles away. I'd hitch the horse up and take him back up Sunday night.

Well, I was coming back and the sun wasn't quite down yet. But it was awful deep snow and, at that time, no snowploughs or the likes o' that. And there was a hill that used to drift in pretty bad and they'd shovel it out. Just the width of a horse and sled down it. The place was shoveled out for to pull in, for to let something pass, if you happened to meet. I saw this little red horse and a sleigh coming towards me. I pulled in one of these places. It was up pretty well towards me then. Well, I looked back again. Not a thing on the road! There was no place it could turn. Not a sign of anything on the road.

Well, there was a fellow lived out back here and he had a little red horse. Exactly the same as that horse. The only thing I ever heard tell of, the horse died in two or three weeks.

I guess 'twas, when I got started, they kept after me to write this. To write that.

> Here's to the Tattrie family, they live back off the street.
> Their place is never tidy and never very neat.
> Ma Tattrie, she's as stubborn as a mule.
> She says that she's married to a darned old fool.

Pa Tattrie, his patience are a few.
You'll sometimes hear him cursing 'til everything is blue.
Sixty-three years of married life, I lived down on the farm
Attending to the cattle they kept down in the barn.

Profits, they were very low and money, it was scarce
But they always had enough to eat 'cause they could
    make it last.
They had thirteen of a family and I am glad to say
That eleven of them are living and feeling very gay.

Laura's the oldest girl, her hair has all turned white
And you can see her coming on a moonlight night.
And there is Lilas, her ears they do hum.
Linda has to do the work when she to the doctor runs.

And now there's Verna, she could out-knit them all
And, when she's not knitting, she's playing with the bowling ball.
Ruby has arthritis and she is almost blind.
Makes me so sorry for her, but then everyone's so kind.

And Jean, the youngest girl, she lives away down east
And when she comes to visit,
    you should see her scrub and sweep.
Audrey, the smallest girl, she never eats no dinner,
    so she can stay this small.
Ronald's the oldest boy. He takes in all the card parties
    they hold down in the hall.

And there's Elroy, he's always in good cheer.
You can see him smiling when he's drinking a bottle of beer.
Freeman lives a few miles away.
When he comes to visit, he hasn't much time to stay.

Now I'll speak of Gary. Politicians he'd like to tame.
If he had the education, he'd be out in the game.
And now, I'll check on Philip, 'cause he grew very tall.
When he goes into the pantry,
    there's no food left in there at all.

And now I'm all through writing. I have no more to say.
I'll fold up my paper and put my pen away.

I got one here, it was read at my daughter's funeral.

'Twas on a Sunday morning, the church it stood so proud.
You could hear her bell aringing so clear and so loud.
And now the people's gathering, they come in from the street.
They're passing in through the door to get themselves a seat.

The minister, she come in. At the pulpit she did stand
And she read the scripture from the bible in her hand.
She preached the sermon of the Saviour on the cross.
If He had not hung and suffered there, well,
        we'd have all been lost.

We know not what He suffered nor what pain He had to bear.
We only know it was for us He hung and suffered there.
And at evening, when the sun was setting low
They took Him down from the cross and laid Him in the tomb.

And three days after, He arose up from the tomb.
He ascended up to heaven to prepare for us a room.
And now, the sermon's over. We bow our heads in prayer.
Dear Lord, will Thou forgive us for the sins we committed here
And take us home to heaven to be in Thy tender care?

And now the choir's singing that hymn we love the best.
Safe in the arms of Jesus, where we get eternal rest.
And now I'm all through writing. I have composed this poem.
We'll follow in His footsteps until He calls us home.

After my daughter died, a few years back, I thought I'd have to write a poem. It hurt pretty bad. So I wrote this one.

In a quiet, country graveyard our daughter Lilas sleeps.
Her soul has gone to heaven to be in God's holy keep.
She left us, oh so sudden, our sorrow it was great.
But we have the pleasure to know
        she's up there with the Great.

She went home to heaven, to be with her son above.
She always thought of him with a mother's love.
She left a large family and their tears did flow
And they still wonder why she had to go.

With God and all His glory, there's all things for the best.
He takes us home to heaven, to eternal rest.
Up there she'll be so happy, for everything's so bright.
'Cause up there in heaven, there never is no night.

And now, as I write these lines, the silent tears they flow.
But, someday, I'll meet her. Someday, I too must go.

I can't complain. I mean, I'm eighty-eight years old and getting around yet. So, I'm thankful for that.

The toe on my left foot, the big toe, the nail in-grew. I had to get it taken off. I had a pretty sore toe afterwards for awhile. But it grew out and it's never bothered me since.

They just freeze the toe then cut it out. The freezing was the only thing. You know, the big toe's kind of a tender thing.

But I think the worst punishment I ever had, I had a small cancer in my nose. I went to the doctor and he stuck a needle right through the end of my nose. That was the worst punishment I ever had.

Here's to Doctor MacCarthy, he always wears a smile.
When he's not in his office, he's jogging for a mile.
He is my family doctor and has been for a number of years.
But, when he gives me a needle, he fills my eyes with tears.

He is a good doctor, he has the healing touch.
But when it comes to saving a life, he can only do so much.
When I go into his office he always seems so kind.
I guess he'll be my doctor 'til I leave this world behind.

I got one in there, "A Walk Down Memory's Lane." On our sixty-fourth anniversary. We were married in Middlebrook, at the wife's home. Cassie's home. That's about six or seven miles from here. We were married in the evening and her sister was married the same time. Was a double wedding. So I made this up on our sixty-fourth anniversary.

Sixty-four years ago tonight I walked in through the door,
Where stood the blushing bride, the one I do adore.
And when the minister he came in, these words I heard him say,
"Do you take this woman to be your wedded wife?"
The answer that I gave to him, "As long as I have life."

And now the wedding's over, you can hear the music play.
And everyone is dancing and feeling very gay.
Now the supper's ready, the plates are piled up high
With sandwiches and wedding cake and good old-fashioned pie.

And now the supper's over, you can hear the guitar hum.
Everyone is dancing, while some are full of rum.
The hands upon the clock, they're moving very fast
And soon you'll hear them say, "This dance will be the last."

And now the guests have all gone home
        to catch up on their rest.
It's up to the bride and groom to do what they think best.
Early in the morning, they hitch the horse up in the sleigh.
They drive from the Millbrook to French River. That's where
        they're going to stay.

And sixty-four years after, they still live on the farm.
They haven't got no cattle, just an empty barn.
And now we're in our eighties, oh how the years did go
And when we're out walking, we're moving very slow.

I've got one more that I should recite to you.

Christmas is all over, the New Year's coming fast.
We all know, three hundred and sixty-five days it will last.
January, the first month of the year.
The snow and cold weather, we'll wish the end was here.

February, the snow is getting deep.
I wish I was like a bear, through winter I could sleep.
And now we're into March, the days are long and bright.
The snow, it is melting and it fills us with delight.

And now it is April, the mud is getting deep.
The traffic on the gravel road, oh, it can only creep.
May, it is a lovely month, the buds on the trees they swell.
And we pick mayflowers, the flower I love to smell.

And now we're into June, the best month of the year.
And we'll plant our gardens, the frost we will be clear.
And now it is July, the weather it is hot.
We're looking for a nice big tree, for a shady spot.

Now we're into August, the days they are still hot.
But we'll pick the beans and peas and cook them in the pot.
Now it is September, the harvest time is here.
The farmers all are busy getting their combines into gear.

Now it is October, the nights are getting cold.
The leaves'll turn their colour to yellow, red and gold.
And now, November, the hunter he will roam
To get himself a nice fat deer to eat when he gets home.

And now it is December, the last month of the year.
Again, we think about Christmas 'cause it is drawing near.
And now, I'm all through writing about the months of the year.
But the months we love the best are the months
        that summer's here.